Mindfulness
At Work

Mindfulness At Work

How to Avoid Stress, Achieve More, and Enjoy Life!

By Dr. Stephen McKenzie

CAREER
PRESS
Pompton Plains, N.J.

MINDFULNESS AT WORK
EDITED AND TYPESET BY DIANA GHAZZAWI

Cover design by Jeff Piasky
Printed in the U.S.A.

To order this title, please call toll-free 1-800-CAREER-1 (NJ and Canada: 201-848-0310) to order using VISA or MasterCard, or for further information on books from Career Press.

The Career Press, Inc.
220 West Parkway, Unit 12
Pompton Plains, NJ 07444
www.careerpress.com

Library of Congress Cataloging-in-Publication Data

McKenzie, Stephen, 1960-

Mindfulness at work : how to avoid stress, achieve more, and enjoy life / by Dr. Stephen McKenzie.

pages cm

Includes bibliographical references and index.

ISBN 978-1-60163-336-1 (alk. paper) -- ISBN 978-1-60163-430-6 (ebook : alk. paper) 1. Job stress. 2. Meditation--Therapeutic use. I. Title.

HF5548.85.M42 2015

158.7'2--dc23

2014028054

To my grandparents, who paved my working way—
Phil, Binnie, Les, and Netta.

Acknowledgments

Thanks to the wonderful team at Exisle for their highly valuable contributions to this book, especially to Benny for helping to shape the idea and to Anouska for polishing it.

Thanks to those who generously gave interviews for the working examples: Michael, Phil, Melanie, Andrew, and Lisa.

And thanks to Melanie and Miranda for their loving sacrifices.

Contents

Chapter 1

What Mindfulness Is and Isn't

*The practice of mindfulness, of bringing the scattered mind home,
and so bringing the different aspects of our being into focus, is called
"Peacefully Remaining," or "Calmly Abiding".... In that setting, we
begin to understand ourselves more, and sometimes even have
glimpses of the radiance of our fundamental nature.*

—Sogyal Rinpoche

Mindfulness isn't what we think it is. Mindfulness isn't anything that we think; it's what we don't think. Mindfulness isn't something that other people do; it's something that we all do. If the only mindful people were the ones doing courses in it or reading books about it or writing books about it, or all three, then humanity wouldn't last very long. We all need to be at least a little bit mindful to get through our days without being hit by the first bus that we mindlessly wander out in front of, or getting hit by the first other totally mindless person whose toes we mindlessly tread on. On a more subtle survival level, being continuously—rather than just occasionally—mindful can help us to get through a day—or even longer—without getting upset by life.

What is mindfulness?

Simply defined, mindfulness is an ancient life-enhancing and healing technique that can help us to remember our natural state of happiness and health, even if we think we are too modern and too busy to prioritize what's really important: being fully alive and fully alive to our full life potential.

However, the essence of mindfulness is, like the essence of *every-thing* else, beyond words. Words are just symbols—models—and sometimes they can get in the way of our understanding, rather than help it, so let's just use the word "mindfulness" as a working construct, a sign-post to a fullness that's beyond words.

Mindfulness can be simmered down (perhaps a better mindfulness metaphor than "boiled"!) into just two active ingredients: awareness and acceptance. These two basic elements of mindfulness can be seen as two wings of a single bird that can fly us higher than we could ever have thought possible, as long as we recognize and use both our wings together. Without acceptance, awareness could be scary; without aware-ness, acceptance could be tranquilizing. When we are aware and when we accept what we are aware of—what's actually happening to us here and now—we are not slaves to our minds and not at war with our lives, and our life circumstances tend to improve.

Being mindful simply means being fully aware, fully able to con-sciously direct our awareness to what is—right here, right now—and fully accepting of what we are aware of. Living and working mindfully is possible for all of us if we can simply let go of our ideas about what we can and can't be. This is our natural state of peace and happiness, and it happens all by itself when we stop getting distracted by what *isn't*—our imaginings of times past and future. The trick to mindfulness, if we be-lieve in the power of tricks, is that it's a lot easier than we think it is.

Most phenomena can be divided into two basic types: man and woman, good cop and bad cop, etc. Mindfulness can also be divided into two types: formal and informal.

Formal mindfulness is the regular practice of a formal mindfulness exercise, which can be described as "meditation," if you're comfortable with this term, or as "the systematic focusing of attention on a particular aspect of sensory reality," if you aren't. We can practice formal mind-fulness in a suit and tie, or a long dress and tiara, depending on our preferences, or we can practice formal mindfulness in any clothes and at any time.

Informal mindfulness just means giving our complete attention to what we are doing and observing our thoughts about it, no matter how we are dressed and no matter how much our mind resists it. Our thoughts can be hard to resist at first, and they can include such sneakily seductive ones as "I have something much better I should be doing!" (than being happy and at peace?), "This isn't working!", or even Bart Simpson's famous "Are we there yet? Are we there yet? Are we there yet?" A valuable practice of informal mindfulness is simply being fully aware of an activity that our minds habitually don't accept, such as washing the dishes, and just doing it, without indulging in the potential mental and physical destructiveness of resisting doing it. If this applied mindfulness exercise seems a bit too strenuous, then you could try the classic mindfulness experiment of eating a raisin while giving your full attention to each of your senses, one by one. If even this seems a bit too challenging, then try it with chocolate!

The good news then is that we can all spend more of our time mindfully happy, peaceful, and healthy, and less of our time, as we habitually and unnecessarily do, being miserably mindless. But practicing mindfulness doesn't mean being mindful all the time. If it did, we would probably all give up on it before it did us any good. Practicing mindfulness actually often involves, especially at first, simply being more frequently mindful of our mindlessness, more aware of our lack of awareness, and more accepting of our non-acceptance, and less frequently judging our judging. If we can even occasionally be conscious of our unconsciousness, then we are making huge progress on our journey to greater happiness and usefulness.

What isn't mindfulness?

Despite what some of us might think about mindfulness, it isn't esoteric or weird or impractical, or something that we need to take on faith or practice in a dark room, or only practice within a religious or philosophical tradition, or need a license for. Perfectly sensible, respectable, and ordinary people formally and informally practice mindfulness (as well as some possibly not quite so sensible, respectable, or ordinary people), and it can help all of us. Hugh Jackman is an internationally successful actor who is based in New York. He is also an extraordinarily ordinary person who practices mindfulness and admits to it on talk shows. Hugh Jackman once gave a plug on *Oprah* for a simple formal mindfulness practice that he does regularly, and which simply consists of giving full awareness to each of our senses, starting with touch and ending with hearing. Hugh described this practice as being simple and natural, and resulting in an increased awareness, which results in him being a better actor and a better parent because he is more connected with his audience and his children.

Unlike some techniques that people sometimes mistake mindfulness for, mindfulness doesn't involve attempting to *change* how we think. Mindfulness actually helps us *transcend* our thinking, especially the thinking that goes around in circles and worries us, by enabling us to focus on and accept what's taking place in our bodies and minds without trying to stop or improve what's happening. Paradoxically, this process often *does* improve our bodies and minds, but this is a fringe benefit rather than a deliberate aim. The aim of mindfulness is to make us more aware of and accepting of our life responses, and to help us observe, rather than be controlled by, our thoughts and feelings. Thoughts and feelings are a natural and positive part of our human lives, but thoughts and feelings that consume and upset us aren't; mindfulness helps us to notice the difference and choose what is useful and beneficial.

Mindfulness isn't a life- and wellness-enhancing practice that we have to accept on faith, or even on the basis of our experience. There's a growing body of scientific evidence that demonstrates that mindfulness can help to treat or manage a wide variety of psychological and physical conditions—such as anxiety, depression, pain, and even cancer—as well as make well people more well.[1] There's also considerable evidence that practicing mindfulness can reduce our chances of developing unwanted subtle psychological or physical manifestations of mindlessness, such as insomnia and unhappiness. Mindfulness is an effective and harmless way of helping us to live our ordinary lives by helping us to learn, make decisions, and communicate optimally. And success in each of these aspects of our lives often results in success in others.

Mindfulness is even being introduced into medical courses, such as the course devised by Dr. Craig Hassed that is now being taught at Monash and Deakin universities in Australia, Auckland University in New Zealand, and Harvard University in the United States. Medical students and their lecturers are increasingly recognizing and valuing the vast potential health benefits of the formal and informal practice of mindfulness—for themselves and for their patients. Once doctors take the health benefits of a wellness-enhancing practice seriously, then it can be seen as being mainstream, because these leaders of public opinion often lead from *behind*!

Ultimately, mindfulness will either help or not help us to live our lives, and acceptance of its benefits doesn't require us to believe in anything other than our own experience. To be mindful, we simply need to have an open mind and heart.

Origins of mindfulness

Mindfulness has been around a long time, probably for as long as there have been people. Ironically, despite its current resurgence, modern mindfulness practices are probably not yet as popularly well-accepted as they were in the ancient cultures where they originated thousands of years ago. (In ancient Indian, Chinese, and other cultures, mindfulness was probably seen as a natural part of people's lives that didn't need to be justified.) It's not known exactly when mindfulness as a formal practice emerged, but there are records of meditation being practiced in China more than 7,000 years ago. Although mindfulness is often associated with Buddhist meditation practices such as *Vipassana*—to see things as they really are—it's an integral aspect of many formal and informal practices that are vital parts of many Eastern and also Western life-knowledge traditions. Eastern mindfulness traditions include Chinese and Indian philosophies/religions such as Taoism, Vedanta, and Buddhism. Western mindfulness-related traditions include ancient Greek philosophy, as described by Pythagoras, Plato, and others, and also the contemplative traditions of Christianity, Judaism, and Sufism (the mystical aspect of Islam).

The sleeping giant of mindfulness practice (and preaching!) has recently awoken in many Western countries after a slumbering consciousness dark age, or at least a dim age. To quote from *Mindfulness for Life* by Doctors McKenzie and Hassed, "This is an overnight lifestyle and clinical sensation that is thousands of years old."[2]

The benefits of mindfulness

William James is regarded as the world's first scientific psychologist, and he was well ahead of this modern time (and well behind an ancient time!) when he said in 1890:

> The faculty of voluntarily bringing back a wandering attention over and over again is the very root of judgment, character, and will. No one is compos sui [mentally competent] if he have it not. An education which should improve this faculty would be the education par excellence. But it is easier to define this ideal than to give practical directions for bringing it about.

Mindfulness can bring home the prodigal son of our wandering attention and give us back our missing-in-action mental competence. Mindfulness can also restore our life essence, something that all too many of us these days can think we've lost!

Mindfulness offers enormous potential benefits for everyone. It can help to restore the mental, physical, and spiritual health and happiness of those of us who are physically, psychologically, or spiritually unwell or unhappy, and also enhance and expand the health and happiness of those of us who are well, more or less. Mindfulness can even help people who have never heard of it (mindfulness pagans) and people who know what it is but who don't believe in it (mindfulness heathens), in the same way that life knowledge and also vitamins can help everyone, not just those of us who believe in them. There are advantages, however, in knowing what mindfulness is, even for those of us who already practice it at least sometimes (and that's all of us) and those of us who benefit from it at least sometimes (and that's also all of us). It's a lot easier to work mindfulness into our life acts if we know what it is at the level of our minds, as well as at the level of our experience.

Have you ever been stressed? If you have, then please read on without delay. If you haven't, then please send us some tips! Stress is the root cause of most human unhappiness—and stress is basically being out of our comfort zone for extended periods. Mindfulness can help us to live our lives more healthily and happily by reducing our stress, and therefore reducing our chances of being sick, miserable, unfulfilled, or all three. Mindfulness can help us to prevent, heal, or learn to live with just about every physical, mental, and psychological malady that can cause us to mislay (never to completely lose) the paradise of our natural human condition, while also making our life a generally richer experience.

We think that stress is caused by events that happen to us *out there*, but actually stress is caused by our minds—and it often ends up in our bodies, and societies of minds and bodies. Stress really comes from how we perceive events, rather than from the events themselves. The same event—losing our job or a relationship—might make us miserable or even happy, depending on how we perceive it:

This is a catastrophe! How can I live without her/him/it?

or

This is terrific! Now that I don't have to live with him/her/it, I'm free!

Actually, we are always free. Free to perceive whatever level of reality we are mindful enough to perceive, and free to realize that our thoughts—even our happiness- and health-destroying ones—are just thoughts. Stress is the root cause of a wide range of psychological, physical, and general life problems such as anxiety, depression, heart disease, and job burnout. Being more mindful can help to prevent and heal many of these problems at their roots by enabling us to step back from uncontrolled and controlling thoughts. Being mindful means simply letting our thoughts come and then go, without reacting to them, without allowing the circus of meaningless mental activity to persuade us that it's more real than we are. We are no longer distracted by the unrealities of what might come to be or what might have been. Instead, we are focused on the reality of what is, here and now.

Mindfulness helps us to be aware of and accept our true self, our universal self that's universally connected and eternal, and not our miserable little idea of our self as cut off and alone. It does this by helping us to be aware of what's actually going on in our bodies and minds, here and now. Unhappiness comes from our thinking that we are unhappy, which basically comes from our thinking too much. When we are mindful, we transcend unhappiness in every area of our lives, because when we are mindful, we transcend our incessant circling, meaningless and destructive thinking processes. All we need to do in any situation to be fully happy, fully fulfilled, and fully alive is to forget what we are not—separate, miserable, obsessed—and remember what we are—mindful, connected, happy, and alive.

Now that we understand what mindfulness is and isn't, the rest of this book will explore and explain how mindfulness works at work by presenting mindfulness's working principles, some key aspects of work that mindfulness can help us do better and more happily, and some working examples.

Take-to-work tips for how mindfulness can help

- We can work at making mindfulness work by being fully aware of the reality of what is—what we can see, hear, feel, smell, taste, and enjoy.

- We can work at *accepting* the reality of what *is*, rather than wishing for what *isn't*, or worrying about what *isn't*.

- We can work at not worrying about not being mindful. Mindfulness often begins with our recognising our mindlessness.

- We can work at going with our mindful flow—we are naturally mindful when we are not trying to be something else.

- We can work at letting go of what our mind *thinks* is important, and connecting with what's *really* important—peace, happiness, and productivity.

Chapter 2

How Mindfulness Can Work at Work

Genius, whatever it be, is like fire in the flint, only to be produced by collision with a proper subject. It is the business of every man to try....
—Dr. Samuel Johnson

One of the most important areas of our lives is our work. Whether we are working officially or unofficially, work is something that we spend a large percentage of our time doing, or putting off doing. This is the nature of our nature. So if mindfulness can practically help us to live our lives, then can it also help us to live our working lives? Does mindfulness work for work? Can mindfulness help us work more naturally, more enjoyably, more harmoniously, and even more productively—for us and for the people with and for whom we work?

The short answer is yes

Mindfulness can work for our work better than a promotion can, or a pay rise, or a new job, or an industrial relations tribunal, or even a family-sized bottle of Prozac. The principles of mindfulness can be applied very successfully to work in general—any work, both paid and unpaid. Mindfulness can help us to transform our working lives into something that really fulfils us, rather than merely something that we have to do or that we are paid to do. It can help us to turn our own job, no matter how apparently challenging or even arduous it might seem, into something that we would do for free, as well as for freedom. So, if you would like to find out how mindfulness can do this and more, please read on.

Know thy need!

You might have thought before reading this book that mindfulness is something that other people do, especially other people who are at least a little bit weird, or who have a particular psychological or physical condition that mindfulness can help to improve. Mindfulness, however, is actually extremely practical and useful for everybody, including us—especially us. The practical benefits of being mindful include being able to work more effectively and enjoyably, and a working knowledge of mindfulness can be an indispensably useful tool of any trade. If we can spend more of our time being mindful, and less of our time being mindless, we can better express who we really are, which is actually much greater than the sum of our working parts. Mindfulness isn't just something that's practiced at home, behind closed doors; it can be taken with us wherever we go, including to work.

Many of our life stresses and strains come from our not knowing who we really are, often because our sense of self can get distorted or confused by our ideas of who we think we are. If we are mindful, then we are living in reality, which means living in the reality of our true potential—both personal and professional. Knowing who we really are, and not just who we think we are, can result in myriad highly practical working advantages, including a better knowledge of what job we can best do and how we can best do it.

There was a famous message inscribed at the entrance to the Oracle of Delphi in ancient Greece: Know Thyself! The working equivalent of this key life instruction, which could be valuably inscribed above the entrance to any workplace, is Know Thy Need! This working wisdom can help us to ask some key work-related questions, as well as some key life-related questions. If we are really fortunate, it can even help us to reach some answers. Perhaps, however, the real answer to any question comes when we realize that we no longer need it.

We don't need complicated answers to our questions about what our job really is or what it's really for. We don't need a degree in industrial relations, a PhD in psychology, or even an operating manual to work out what we are really working on, with whom, and for whom. All we need to know to successfully start, finish, and enjoy any work is the need we need to meet—and this includes knowing what the real purpose of our work is. If our job is selling hamburgers, then the need that we need to meet might seem quite simple: to feed hamburgers to a hamburger-hungry world. If we are mindful of a deeper reality, however, then we might realize that our customers actually need something more than the hamburger they have lined up to buy—and that doesn't just mean fries!

If our job is selling hamburgers, maybe our customers' real need is for a sense of connectedness, of being appreciated for the unique and wonderful individual that they truly are and not just as the next body and wallet in our line. If that sounds like too much to give somebody in a hamburger line or to anybody else, and you would prefer to recommend a place down the road where they offer much more than mere hamburgers, then try thinking more deeply about what people's real needs might be in any situation. Maybe the next person in the hamburger line or our fellow CEO of a multinational company with whom we are trying to clinch a billion-dollar deal both really need to feel listened to, valued, connected, and truly human. Maybe they need to feel this rather than like an exploited or ignored means to our end—a way for us to make a dollar or a billion dollars out of them with as little bother as possible.

Maybe the best beginning of a successful billion-dollar or two-dollar working relationship is to really listen to the person with whom we are dealing, to smile at them, to find out something about what it feels like to be them. We already have a great working model of this; we know what it's like to be any human being because we know what it's like to be us.

Seven general mindfulness working principles

These general mindfulness working principles can help us do everything in our lives more peacefully, happily, and productively—even our work. If we put these principles into practical practice, then we can better understand whether our working situation is the best expression of who we really are and, if it isn't, how to improve it.

1. Self-knowledge

This above all: to thine own self be true
And it must follow, as the night the day
Thou canst not then be false to any man
—William Shakespeare, *Hamlet*

What's the benefit, for me and my work, of knowing who I really am? This is a perfectly legitimate question, and there's a perfectly legitimate answer to it! If we don't know who we really are, then we risk getting destructively attached to what we think we are. This can mean getting destructively identified with our ideas of ourselves, including our ideas about our roles or parts—including our working parts. We might, for example, think and believe "I am a plumber," or "I am a teacher," or "I am a rocket scientist," which is fine, as long as we don't become so identified with this description of ourselves that we forget our deeper selves. Identifying with who we think we are can mean that, in much the same way that a professional actor can get lost in his or her role, we forget our whole.

When we do any work mindfully, the work can be a valuable reminder to us of our true freedom—our pure consciousness. Whether we work as a butcher or a baker or a rocket-ship maker—or a lawyer, a salesperson, or even an actor—we will soon end up typecast if we identify too strongly with our role. We have a great opportunity in life to play our true role truly and then let it go. Work can help us more than anything else to realize that we are more than the sum of our working parts.

Socrates and Plato were a famous ancient Greek philosophical superstar double act (Socrates spoke, Plato wrote). One of their key ideas forms the active ingredient of many wisdom traditions. According to Socrates and Plato, there is "the formless"—an absolute—and there are forms that arise in this formlessness and then return to it. These forms include our thoughts, our bodies, and our jobs, and we can get stuck in them if we mindlessly believe in the reality of this unreality. This would be like someone in a movie theater getting so caught up in the movie that they forget that it's just a movie and start screaming out earnest advice to an actor on the screen, "Look out, there's a dinosaur chasing you!"

According to Socrates and Plato, and many other reputable wisdom traditions, suffering comes from the illusion that the fleeting forms that we can get so hung up on are permanent, and that therefore the show is the substance. To transcend our suffering, including our working suffering, all we need to do is simply realize that what seems either painful or pleasurable won't last long, so we can just enjoy the show and do what we need to do to make our life work.

The ancient wisdom traditions that gave us mindfulness practices also gave us the highly valuable working knowledge that we all have a unique talent—all seven billion of us—as well as the knowledge that we are far more than we can describe. Discovering our true and unique talent—our natural role—is a vital part of our life's work, although this is often unrecognized. Socrates and Plato gave us the hot working life tip that "an unexamined life is not worth living." This doesn't mean that we have to pass an examination before we can go on to our next job, but rather to be the best person that we can be, we need to live life mindfully enough—consciously enough—to discover who we really are and how we can best express it, including through our work.

Despite the proliferation in modern times of career counseling and careers, we have too much work choice and too little reason to choose. According to an ancient Indian wisdom tradition, infants were once given a collection of particular work-related toys and invited to choose some to play with. The child's choice was respected as revealing their deep professional talent and interest, which was then nurtured. In modern times, the psychologist and philosopher Abraham Maslow developed a theory of "self-actualization." This theory basically states that to be truly happy, we need to feel that we are expressing who we truly are, that we are playing the part that we were born to play.

To be fully mindful in our lives and in our working lives, we need to recognize that our roles, including our working roles, are just roles, and therefore parts of the whole us. We are infinitely more than our infinite parts, and we are infinitely connected to others, including to those with whom we have working relationships.

2. Unity

No man is an island, entire of itself; every man is a piece of the continent, a part of the main.
—John Donne

Can being mindful of our vital connection to others help us to work better and more enjoyably? Ultimate working knowledge comes when we are mindful, when we are fully aware, alive, and connected. Then we can act optimally and ultimately successfully in our jobs, and we can choose jobs that allow us to act optimally and successfully. This working mindfulness can also help us to recognize our true selves by helping us to recognize our connection with others.

There are people living and working in modern Africa who still live and work in the ancient Ubuntu wisdom tradition. The traditional Ubuntu response to the question "Are you well?" is "I am well if you are well!" There are people living and working in modern India, Nepal, and elsewhere who still live and work according to the ancient Indian Vedic wisdom tradition. They greet each other with the word "Namaste," which means "The universal within me recognizes the universal within you." Ultimately, all working harmony and also all morality comes from our recognizing our integral links with others, and there are versions of this recognition in all of the world's great wisdom traditions, such as the New Testament's "Do unto others as you would have them do unto you." We gain happiness by giving it; similarly, working with others is actually the best way to work for ourselves.

A highly practical example of the working usefulness of unity is teamwork. We all know that a champion team will beat a team of champions any day or night, and this is because of their unity. The Geelong Australian Rules football team is a good example of a sporting team successfully using working unity. Shortly before entering a highly successful phase in its history, the Geelong football team consciously employed practices that would help them bond together as a unit, such as yoga, which helps to reduce friction by harmonizing bodies, minds, and spirits. After this conscious commitment, the Geelong football team showed marvelous free-flowing football teamwork—unity—and achieved great on-field success. Many other sports teams have used mindfulness principles successfully, and these techniques are regularly employed by sports psychologists and other helpful experts, even though they are often not described in mindfulness terms. The practical benefits of unity apply to working teams and life teams, as well as to sports teams.

3. Truth

In matters of truth and justice, there is no difference between large and small problems, for issues concerning the treatment of people are all the same.

—Albert Einstein

Truth comes from open-mindedness, which can lead to vast successes that we can't achieve when we are not open to our true opportunities. An open mind allows us to recognize that truth can truly be found anywhere—in a book on mindfulness, in an episode of *The Simpsons*, or even in the words of somebody with whom we don't agree. To be open-minded is to be prepared to be proven wrong and to work toward *the* truth rather than *my* truth. When Socrates said that he knew nothing, he wasn't accusing the Athenian education system of incompetence; he was saying that we can't learn anything if we think we know everything. There is the story of the university professor who went to visit a well-known Zen philosopher. The Zen master poured him tea and kept pouring until the professor's cup literally overflowed. Then the Zen master told the protesting professor that he couldn't learn anything with his over-full mind that let in nothing new. If we have an open mind, we can see a better way of doing any job, even if somebody else suggests it.

4. Awareness

Do not dwell in the past. Do not dream of the future.
Concentrate the mind on the present moment.

—Gautama the Buddha

Work can be a wonderful opportunity for us to maintain our awareness, to consistently connect with and focus on something useful, and therefore develop deeper levels of mindfulness, of consciousness. There's an old saying that when a wise man (or woman) fetches water (or even wine), they just fetch water (or even wine); when they chop wood, they just chop wood. This might seem simple, but it's also profound, and real profundity is often revealed in simplicity. Think about how well we might fetch water, chop wood, hammer in a nail, wash a dish, or clinch a billion-dollar deal if we are thinking about how well or badly our team did last week, or about how much the person with whom we are on water-fetching or billion-dollar-deal-clinching duty pleases or displeases us. Chances are that we will both get wet! Consider what might happen to us if we chop wood or slice sushi without awareness!

Most of us aren't enrolled in formal mindfulness programs, but most of us are enrolled in formal work programs. Our work is a great opportunity for us to work toward our ultimate happiness, meaning, and peace by simply staying tuned into, rather than out of, whatever we are working on. A fringe benefit of being mindful at work is that it can help us to be more mindful during all our life activities. If we are fully with the present moment—and not against it, distracted by thoughts of other moments—we can perform any job well, and this can awaken our full working and life potential.

5. Service

Would you like anything else?
—The (hypothetical) General Sales Manual

Service is probably about as sexy as asparagus, but they are both deeply good for us, and they can both give us deeply enjoyable experiences, if we embrace them like a thistle—so hard that we feel their love and not their prickles! Our happiness and peace of mind increases, as well as our professional success, when we genuinely serve others, when we genuinely give something to them, when we genuinely connect with them through meeting their need and not through meeting our idea of their need.

Our motivation is the key to how well we will do any job, and it's vital that our motivation is to meet the needs of the person with whom or for whom we are working, rather than meeting our own ideas about our own needs at the expense of the person we are serving. We might have trouble with words such as "service," "surrender," and "devotion" because they can suggest to our minds that we will lose something by practicing them, but what we are really surrendering through serving others is the need to be an island. This then lets us fully connect with others and therefore with our true selves. Ice cream might seem more appealing than asparagus, just as self-service might seem more appealing than serving others. According to some highly reputable and practical ancient wisdom traditions, however, what seems like nectar can soon turn into poison, and what seems like poison can soon turn into nectar.

Paradoxically, there are things that we get more of when we give them away, and these include love, attention, and service. We get more of all of these by giving them away, and nothing will prove this better to us than mindful service will. Giving service grudgingly or without attention isn't real service at all, and it isn't really useful to anybody. Service is our great opportunity to meet our own real need by meeting the needs of others, and the key to service is listening to people and not to our perhaps prejudiced (pre-judged, pre-packaged) ideas about them.

Whether or not service is good or bad depends on whether it's provided with care and attention. We probably all remember situations when we've gone into a shop and bought a selection of particularly worthy, wisdom-enhancing books, or even a slice of pizza and a can of Coke, and then been charged 10 times what they should have cost by a shop assistant who appeared to be giving more attention to their bubble gum and dreams than to us! We probably all also remember situations when we were served by someone who cared about us enough to connect with us and who offered us even more service than we hoped for. We probably also all remember which of these situations we liked better and who we would be more likely to offer our return business.

6. Reason

Reason is the ability to discern the transient from the eternal,
the changing from the unchanging.
—Shankara

Reason is going out of fashion even faster than talking to people rather than texting them is, but it can be highly valuable to us professionally as well as personally because it can help us to work in line with everyone's best interests, and not just in line with our ideas of our own best interests or our employer's best interests. Reason relates to service because there's actually a good reason for serving others (just as there is for talking to them), and this is that our welfare and happiness is closely connected to that of other people. We are in this play called life together.

Reason relates to justice because our actions that are good for everyone are just and our actions that aren't good for everyone are unjust. It's therefore practically important that we act on a broader basis than how we can best make a dollar, or a lot of dollars, or best look important. Acting on the basis of reason, rather than blind selfishness, will eventually result in our getting more of everything anyway. Reason has fringe benefits that are neither taxable nor taxing.

Two particularly practical examples of the benefits of using reason in the workplace are workplace safety and industrial relations, where the long-term welfare of everyone who makes up a workplace is considered and acted on.

7. Wonder

From wonder into wonder, existence opens.

—Lao Tzu

Can wonder be useful in our work? The international mindfulness expert Ellen Langer described novelty as the key to a mindful existence, and this means seeing things as if for the first time. It can be wonderful and also productive to experience all aspects of our lives as brand new, including our working lives. In order to do anything beautifully, joyfully, and truthfully, we need to be enthusiastic, we need to love, and we need to experience wonder.

It's possible for us to spend our entire working lives dragging our bodies and minds out of bed and into their place of employment, and then dragging them through the same weary and repetitive actions that we dragged them through yesterday. It's also possible to get out of bed like we are getting out of jail free, and see the wonder in both our work and the people with whom we work. It's possible to have either of these very different experiences in the same job and on the same day. To remember the wonder of life, and of our working life, we need to let go of our ideas about our jobs and just do them—wonderfully.

A practical example of the potential work-related benefits of wonder is the working life of the spectacularly dysfunctional hotel owner Basil Fawlty in the classic 1970s English TV show, *Fawlty Towers*. This show was actually, surreptitiously, a mindfulness training guide, of course, and it was based on the intrinsically funny as well as educational situation of someone who doesn't like people, or serving them, working in a job where it's extremely difficult to avoid both. Basil Fawlty gloriously displayed all of the seven deadly mindless work sins in his job as a hotel manager by simultaneously lacking self-knowledge, unity, truth, awareness, service, reason, and wonder. A wonderfully instructive thing about Basil Fawlty is that he could have made his life work much better for others and himself by forgetting his life's stresses and remembering its wonder. Any job, any life, is wonderful if we can remember to experience it and its opportunities in our natural state of wonder.

Seven specific mindfulness working principles

As well as the seven general working principles of mindfulness listed previously, there are also seven important and valuable specific ones. These principles underlie key practical techniques that help us to achieve and maintain mindfulness at work.

1. Begin all work in stillness

Have you ever noticed that when things go wrong at work, it's often because they started off wrong? Maybe we were in such a hurry to get things done that we forgot to listen to our instructions. Maybe we were in such a hurry to get an amazingly good result in the future that we forgot to attend to what we were doing right now. There's a saying: "More haste, less speed," and this means that we can accomplish things at work more efficiently and more quickly when we are really focused on what we are working on. The key to our job success isn't what we do in our job, but what we do in our preparation for it. Stillness is a vital part of mindfulness, and it's a portal to inner calm and focus as well as to outer success.

2. Separate the components of our work with pauses

Reconnecting with our natural stillness during our work is as important as starting our work in stillness. Most of us informally practice mindfully pausing and reconnecting with the stillness that underlies all activity, whether we notice it or not. This informal practice can involve stopping work to have a cup of tea, or possibly something much less good for us. These pauses between activities are natural and necessary and are the working equivalent of punctuation in written prose; withoutpausesouractivitieswillblurintoeachother!

3. Work until our work is finished

This principle might seem obvious, but just because something is obvious doesn't mean it isn't true. We can easily forget to finish what we've started if we are tired or distracted, and if we forget to work until we are finished, it's hard to stay mindful. It's easy to be seduced by our greatest tempter—our minds—into thinking that we can finish our task another time, and it can be easy for us to accumulate drawers full of "another times." There's a principle known as "the last inch." This principle refers to how the last part of our job can be the hardest, but this is often its most important part, our real working rite of passage. The sporting equivalent to the last inch is the last or championship lap, which is often the most challenging and the most vital.

4. Meet our working need

It's very easy with any job we do to just do what we think needs to be done, or what we would like to do, or what we think somebody else would like us to do. It's important, however, for us to stay focused, awake, and connected with others enough to do what needs to be done. The key to doing what needs to be done is to really listen to the people with whom and for whom we are working. This means being open to the possibility that what they really need isn't what we think they need.

5. Allow our instrument to do the work

This doesn't just mean allowing our tools to do their job without straining to achieve a result through them. It also means allowing the people with whom or for whom we are working to do their job. It's easy for us to lose so much consciousness that we see others merely as vehicles for our speeding egos. Recognizing and letting go of this thought pattern can be liberating—for us and others. To do this, we need to trust that the working truth is enough, and that we don't need to help it along by trying so hard that we strain our working relationships. Allowing the natural results of our efforts to blossom without forcing results or snatching at them can be a powerful exercise in workplace awareness and acceptance. Optimally expressing our nature through our work often means allowing others to optimally express their nature through their work.

6. Focus on where our work is taking place

This principle is the working equivalent of keeping our eyes on the ball when we play a sport, so that we don't drop what's important to us. If we can focus our attention on the point where our bodies and minds make contact with what we are working on, then we will truly connect with what we are doing and work harmoniously. Working optimally requires our full-focused attention to be on our task, and working optimally also develops our full-focused attention. You might like to try an experiment. Do some work that you would probably normally avoid, such as washing some particularly dirty dishes or dogs, or serving something to somebody that you would rather throw at them. Now try doing this same task with your attention fully engaged—really feel the dish or the dog, or really hear the sound of your disagreeable customer's voice. Is it boring or objectionable or second rate? Is anything boring or objectionable or second rate if we give it our full attention? Try doing a working life experiment and find out!

7. Let our work flow

If we are digging a ditch or performing intricate open-heart surgery, it can seem like we are doing what we are doing. It can also seem like the result of doing what we are doing is vitally important, or that we really need to please someone or avoid failing, for another day at least. This idea of feeling caught up in what we are working on, and attachment to its results, actually makes our work harder than it needs to be, resulting in suffering. We are essentially the observer of a mind and a body that does the work, and this deep working reality doesn't just apply to the perhaps apocryphal three out of four council workers who lean on their spades observing the fourth worker work! This deep working reality doesn't even just apply to the perhaps apocryphal highly paid CEOs of major companies whose profits improve while they are on leave. This deep working reality means that our habitual preoccupation with the rewards of our work causes us to lose our working focus, which leads to inefficiency and disorder.

Our deep essence doesn't have a separate identity and therefore doesn't really have anything to work for or against. Working effectively, truly, and happily means working for love and to meet needs, and not working for reward or results. Work rewards come naturally when we are non-attached and focused on our job, and when we are not stuck in the anxious ideas of reality that our minds superimpose on reality.

We don't have to work as Boxer, the work-life unbalanced horse worked in George Orwell's *Animal Farm*: harder and harder until we end up packed off to the glue factory by our sadistic and ungrateful employer! The *Bhagavad Gita* is a great philosophical book from an ancient wisdom tradition that is also a mindful work manual. It's an allegorical story about an ordinary guy and god setting off to work in a great battle, as a metaphor for all of our lives and jobs, even if they aren't quite as glamorous. The main message in this life manual is that if we work without attachment to results, then we are working our way to freedom rather than to tyranny. If we let go of the fruits of our actions and just act—truthfully and joyfully—then we will be free of the uncertainty of never knowing whether our work and life results will be good or bad, and we will be free of the selfishness that comes from an attitude of "What's in it for me?" What's really in work for me and for others is a naturally wonderful opportunity to do what we love, and to love what we do.

Take-to-work tips for how mindfulness can work at work

- Less can be more. When we are conscious enough to stop and consider what we really need to be doing in our work, we can work a lot more efficiently, productively, and enjoyably.
- Our work is greater than the sum of its working parts. We will work better when we are mindful enough to realize who we really are and why we are really working on what

we are working on. We are all working on being the best that we can be...together.

- Things often work out well at work if we just let them be what they are and not want them to be what they aren't.

- Whatever it is that we are working on, if we do it with our complete attention and acceptance, then we will do it mindfully and we will do it well.

Chapter 3

Mindful Decision-Making at Work

It is in your moments of decision that your destiny is shaped.
—Anthony Robbins

What makes a great decision great and a terrible decision terrible? What was the best decision you ever made? What was the worst? What was the difference in the process that led to your best and worst decisions? If you've thought of a good decision you've made—recent or not so recent—then what led to it? Have you ever made a good decision after worrying all night about what you should do? Have you ever made a bad decision after simply knowing what you should do without even thinking about it?

Like most things, decisions can be big or small, and their results can be big or small. You might be able to think of an example of what seemed like a big result following what seemed like a small decision, and also an example of what seemed like a small result following what seemed like a big decision. Regardless of how big or small it seems at the time, our making the right decision can seem enormously important—so important that our life depends on our getting it right or, even worse, that other people's lives depend on it or, worse still, that our working lives depend on it.

Maybe what we see as the enormous responsibility of our making the right decisions can even lead us to consider giving up our role as the CEO of an enormous company that we think needs us to constantly get our large and important decisions right, or to consider giving up our role as the co-CEO of a husband-and-wife work team whose decision-making seems even more important. Maybe our constant need to make important working decisions as well as other life decisions has resulted in us at least occasionally being tempted to demote ourselves and join the lucky billions of workers who seem to just follow orders and not get into trouble if the decision that they follow isn't the "right" one—"I was just following orders!" But can we really avoid making decisions? And should we avoid making decisions even if we can?

Alan Watts was an Englishman who helped popularize Eastern philosophy/religions such as Buddhism and Taoism in America and beyond in the 1950s, '60s, and '70s. A self-described "spiritual entertainer" rather than an official expert in workplace decision-making, he nevertheless helped to make philosophy work for everyone—even workers—by applying it to real life. He gave a talk once in California where he illustrated the potential working hazards of decision-making with a story about an exceptional worker. The exceptional worker was a farmhand who could do in a day what most other workers took two days to do and, even better, he didn't ask questions; he just worked! This exceptional worker not only worked quickly and independently, but he also worked cheaply and happily, and his new boss soon grew to love him. Then one day the boss asked his new star worker to do a new job that he thought he would romp through.

"You see that pile of potatoes over there?"

"Yes."

"All I want you to do is sort through them, and make three smaller piles: a pile of the best potatoes, a pile of the worst potatoes, and a pile of the middle quality potatoes."

"Okay."

After a day of potato sorting the star worker quit. "I'm happy milking cows or putting up fences or even driving your wife into town to do her shopping, but this is just too much—decision after decision after decision!"

This story is reminiscent of one told to me by an old and dear family friend who was intrigued by a young man she knew telling her that he didn't envy the new job of an acquaintance who had just successfully completed a two-day course in holding up either a "slow" sign for oncoming traffic or a "stop" sign, depending on the circumstances. The young man thought that this was a hideously stressful job because of its decision-making demands. These stories about the potential hazards of decision-making are reminiscent of the ongoing decision-making demands on judges and chairs of medical research grant-making organizations, hairdressers, and people in many other constant decision-making occupations—who gets what, when, and on what basis? Maybe we can't all quit our jobs that require constant decision-making, or quit our decision-making, but maybe we can give up our stressful decision-making attitudes. Maybe we can make decisions more mindfully and therefore more easily, naturally, peacefully, and successfully; this includes being more mindful of why we are making them.

Mindless decision-making models

It is only in our decisions that we are important.

—Jean-Paul Sartre

There are as many mindless models of decision-making as there are mindless minds. Mindless decision-making is characterized by some very common traits: haste, attachment to a particular result, not listening, and excessive emotion (particularly negative emotions such as pride, revenge, greed, and anger). Not surprisingly, these are the opposite of mindful traits! There are many real-life examples of high-profile mindless decisions being made by high-profile people, but listing some of these as examples here is inappropriate for many reasons, including a need to be mindful of potential lawsuits! It's better, therefore, to provide some fictional examples of mindless decision-making.

Shakespeare gave us plenty of examples of just about everything worth taking note of, and this certainly includes mindless decision-making. Macbeth was the CEO of a large 11th-century organization known as the Scottish region of Cawdor. Macbeth expanded his family business (of lording it over peasants, etc.) by acquiring a neighboring organization known as the Scottish region of Glamis—this was a lordly performance bonus that was bestowed on him by the overall CEO of his overall organization, King Duncan of Scotland. While being CEO of what was now quite a substantial Scottish regional business—Cawdor and Glamis, Inc.—might have satisfied the leadership aspirations of many ambitious regional CEOs, even Macbeth, it certainly didn't satisfy his partner (in business, life, and crime), Lady Macbeth.

Lady Macbeth decided that Macbeth and her family lording business needed to dramatically increase its profits (such as annual peasant production) by vastly expanding its operations. There was an impediment, however, to the professional expansion of Cawdor and Glamis, Inc., and this impediment was King Duncan of Scotland. The rest of the story is, of course, history.

All of Shakespeare's plays contain great human messages, and these often relate to the considerable difficulties into which mindless decision-making can lead us. The great mindful decision-making lesson that we can learn from Macbeth is that when we lose our awareness of the true value of what we are and what we have, including our connections with others, we can be exposed to the dangers of making mindless decisions that will come back to haunt us (like a mindless hungry ghost at the feast of our consciousness).

Macbeth's murderous business-expansion decision to kill King Duncan haunted him literally as well as psychologically and gave us the expression "the ghost at the feast" (in the form of Macbeth's erstwhile friend and lordly business comrade Banquo). Duncan's murder symbolizes the murder of truth and was motivated by negative emotions such as greed. This is a similar story to many other famous ones in literature and life, such as Goethe's story of Dr. Faustus, who makes a diabolical deal in which he sacrifices his eternal soul for some short-term material gains. Decisions to sacrifice something large and lasting (our true wealth) for something small and fleeting (our perceived profits) are always mindless, because if we were fully aware, fully conscious, fully human, we wouldn't make them.

Another famous historical example of mindless decision-making that no amount of hand washing could rectify was Pontius Pilate's decision to wash his hands of the execution of Jesus. As with Lady Macbeth, who famously could never successfully wash Duncan's blood off her hands, Pontius Pilate's "action" could never be cleaned up. Sometimes we mindlessly choose inaction simply by not mindfully choosing action.

A final example of mindless decision-making, or non-making, is more modern. Homer Simpson and his entire family are great modern examples (if perhaps negative ones) of life and working wisdom (or the lack of it). Homer once went up a mountain in India with the Indian owner of a local convenience store. On top of their destiny mountain was a great sage who could reputedly answer any question accurately. A decision needed to be made as to what questions to ask the sage. The convenience store proprietor decided on many excellent questions about how to better run his life and convenience business. Homer didn't decide on any questions at all, but he somehow got in first, leading to a conversation that went something like this:

"Are you the great Indian mountain sage?"

"Yes, you can ask me any three questions you like and I will answer them."

"Are you sure that you're really the great sage?"

"Yes, quite sure."

"And you can really answer any three questions?"

"Yes, I can."

"Then what about..."

"I have already answered your three questions. Goodbye!"

What links the above extremely diverse examples of mindless decision-making is the common non-recognition of a connection between us and those with whom we are dealing, and a corresponding lack of connection with our reason and deep life knowledge. Mindless decision-making models could be summarily described as "What's in it for me?"

This approach is similar to the utilitarian philosophy that emerged in the 19th century, which is pragmatically based on the idea that happiness for all of us isn't a realistic option. According to this life/business philosophy, we should therefore make decisions that bring the greatest happiness to the greatest number of people, which often lead to there not being much of anything left for the excluded minority.

Mindful decision-making models

Never cut a tree down in the wintertime. Never make a negative decision in the low time. Never make your most important decisions when you are in your worst moods. Wait. Be patient. The storm will pass. The spring will come.
—Robert H. Schuller

There's really only one model of mindful decision-making. Mindful decisions are simple, just as mindfulness is simple, and mindful decision-making simply means making decisions when we are awake—to all of our and everyone's opportunities. Henry Ford's Model T business decision that customers could have "any color as long as it's black" is a great example of mindful decision-making, not because it made him vast amounts of money, but because it was inspired by his mindful ability to recognize and meet a very real need for a practical and inexpensive car that wasn't influenced by the arbitrary complexities of fashion.

There are many other real-life positive examples of mindful and successful decisions made in the business world and beyond. These examples include the vastly successful decision of Bill Gates to implement and market a complex operating system in his computers that is amazingly user-friendly simply because it matches how the human mind works: by seeing and choosing (clicking). Bill Gates made a very different, but perhaps even more mindful, decision to direct some of his vast business profits into some highly useful medical research, including ways of reducing malaria-related harm. (Malaria kills more people worldwide than any other disease, including cancer.)

A beautifully human example of mindful decision-making is described in the words of Charles Dickens, and given magnificent life by the actor Ronald Colman in the 1935 classic film *A Tale of Two Cities*: "It is a far, far better thing I do than I have ever done; it is a far, far better rest that I go to than I have ever known...."

Ronald Colman's character was Sydney Carton, an Englishman embroiled in the French Revolution, who substituted himself for another man who was about to be guillotined because he decided that this other man's life was more valuable than his own. Perhaps we can all work toward making more consistently mindful decisions by increasingly recognizing reality and our true place in it. Maybe we can even be mindful of what the results of our next decision—large or small—would look like on a film screen!

Mindful decision-making can be summarized by the Three Musketeers' working model: All for one and one for all! An earlier version of this comes from ancient Indian Vedic philosophy:

> May all be happy
>
> May all be without disease
>
> May all be free of suffering of any kind.

What motivates our decisions?

Act as if what you do makes a difference. It does.

—William James

How happy we ultimately are with the process and results of our decisions will depend greatly on what motivated them. Are we motivated by what Daniel Goleman described in *Emotional Intelligence* as the main motivations for most people in high-level management positions: a desire for prestige, power, or profit?[1] Or are we motivated by a recognition of who we truly are and how we can best express this in our work and therefore allow others to express their true selves in their work? What motivates us to do anything that we do, and to make any choices that we make, will greatly affect our eventual state of mind or mindfulness, and

our state of mind is actually a far more important consequence of anything that we decide to do, or not do, than is our idea about the eventual
rewards or costs.

Probably none of us consciously decides to stay up all night worrying
about a decision that we have to make. Probably none of us consciously
postpones fully connecting with, and therefore fully enjoying, our family or work relationships until we made a decision. Which of the seemingly equally well-qualified candidates to join my company do I hire?
Which of the seemingly equally well-qualified candidates to leave my
company do I fire? What do I do next? Should I ask my supervisor about
whether I'm slicing my sushi too thinly, or should I show some initiative
and make my own decision? What if I get it wrong? Should I take an apparently good offer made by the representative of a large Tokyo abalone
consortium for the multi-million-dollar abalone business that I'm man-
aging director of, or should I ring the owners in the middle of the night
and ask them what to do? Should I show initiative or caution?

Our decisions can be motivated by the superficialities of what ap-
pears to be or they can be motivated by the deeper realities of what really
is—what is really needed by me, my company, my customer, my boss.
Are there really half-a-dozen seemingly competing needs or is there just
one, such as the need to be listened to? Mindless decisions tend to be
motivated by a perceived self-interest that often conflicts with a deeper self-interest, and they tend to result in consequences that ultimately
aren't good for anybody. If we all decide to act in isolation, we will eventually find unity in our mutual suffering.

Mindful decisions are motivated by our deep connectedness with
the rest of our world and who or what's in it that collectively forms our
greater selves. Mindless decisions are motivated by what seems to be
important, whether this is profit or expansion or expedience. The technical difference between being a good witch and a bad witch lies in the
differing motivations. Good magic is performed for others—our greater
selves; bad magic is performed for ourselves—our lesser selves. It's the
same with any form of power, be that our million-dollar-deal-making

power or our sushi-making power: it doesn't matter how much we have; it does matter how wisely we wield it.

We could try to individually make mindful decisions, or we could just continually act from a deep motivation to connect with and create, rather than to divide and destroy. There's a saying derived from ancient Vedic wisdom: "Don't avoid mistakes [bad decisions]; avoid conditions that are conducive to mistakes." We can remove the root cause of our bad decisions, and the suffering that they lead to, when we remove our sense of separation, when we are motivated by our connection and not by our division.

Is it better to make a bad decision now or a good decision later?

Last week's meeting of the procrastination society is today cancelled.
—Anonymous graffiti

Mindless decisions are often made so fast that they're hasty, but they can also be so slow that they're non-existent. Both tortoises and hares can be mindless. Hares are often mindless (hare-brained) when they move so quickly that they can't remember what they're rushing to or from. Tortoises can be mindless when they move so slowly that they go to sleep.

A common response to our believing that we don't know what to do next—whether this is because we see too many good options or not enough, or because we are overwhelmed by our mind's perceived scary consequences of our decision—is to delay our decision. This abandonment of all action but worry can paralyze us in many areas of our lives, including our working lives. The fear of the consequences of a bad decision can have far worse consequences than the decision itself would if this fear results in us doing nothing but agonizing about what could have been. Maybe in this state of moribund mindlessness, we will put off applying for a new and better job until the applications close, or maybe we will put off making a decision that will allow us to appropriately expand our professional opportunities until those opportunities are snatched from us by a more cutting-edge focused competitor. Procrastination is not only the thief of time, but also of our peace of mind. We often get surprisingly good, surprisingly quickly, at things that we do frequently—this is what makes our habits so powerful—and this principle applies to our inactions as well as our actions. So what do we do about our "not doing"?

Mindful decision-making begins with the recognition of our need to act. Life wouldn't be life if we didn't decide to live it, constantly. Every day of our lives begins with a decision to get up and face the day. If we are mindful, we can decide not only to face the day, but also to fully experience its full potential—and this includes workdays! An old man in a bar once told me that he thought I looked like a philosopher. (I'm still not sure whether this was an insult or a compliment!) He then told me that he would give me a philosophical thought to try on for size: "Life is a holiday from oblivion!"

The *Bhagavad Gita* offers some potentially vital life and working life improvement tips, as it's all about the mind problems encountered by its hero when he can't make a decision to act. The story is a metaphor for all of our decision-making problems. In the *Bhagavad Gita*, a great ancient prince called Arjuna was paralyzed with doubt and anxiety. His lands were under siege by a group of noblemen who had turned rotten—motivated entirely by the need for ever-expanding princely profits—and he had to decide what to do about them. We are all faced with situations every day where we have to decide whether to act or not act, and how. The *Bhagavad Gita* could just as easily be written in a modern form where the greed-crazed invaders are workplace, rather than princely, villains.

Before he was paralyzed by doubt about what to do next, Prince Arjuna was a great CEO. He had made just and timely decisions that were motivated by a desire for all to share the wealth of the kingdom—knowledge and material—but on this particular day, he was in a pickle. One miserably misty morning on a hill near Kurukshetra, Prince Arjuna found himself at the head of a mighty army, facing an even mightier one on the opposing hill. Battle conches were blaring and his army was ready to live or die gloriously, but Prince Arjuna wasn't. Luckily, he just happened to have a particularly wise god as his charioteer, Krishna. Actually this wasn't dumb luck at all, because Arjuna had managed to make one great decision before he froze: to choose Krishna's offer of his guidance (wisdom) rather than his army (power). To summarize what happened next and to divert slightly from the original Sanskrit and its usual English equivalent:

I just can't do it, Krishna! These guys are my relatives—I can't fight them. I can't kill them. I don't care that they've turned rotten and just want power for power's sake. Hell, who doesn't these days? And yet if I don't fight them, we'll all end up in a dark age and then what will inspire Bollywood movies in a few thousand years? What will I do?

Krishna's answer took up over 20 verses of one of the world's great wisdom manuals, but it can be summarized as: "You simply have to do what deep down you know is right. Stuff the consequences!"

In the workplace, if like Arjuna, we're too paralyzed by doubt to do it or do it well, we could start with deeply reflecting on what we're supposed to be working on. Our reflection may lead to our realizing that we need to do a different job or do this one differently. We might, for example, be able to do our job more freely, successfully, and enjoyably if we realize that our problems are caused by our mind-made resistance to something deeper than our job situation, such as to being told what to do. When we stop wasting energy on agitating about what we are doing, or not doing, we can be in a much better position to transcend it. We can do this by getting a different job—possibly one working for ourselves—or we can transcend our working problem by changing our mindset, so that we work with others rather than for them or even against them. Unconsciously resisting work can be even more damaging to us and others than unconsciously starting it. Working is a wonderful way of doing our best in life and of working out what our best is.

There's a time to act and a time to not act, but whatever we decide to do, our decision needs to be conscious and it needs to be motivated by

what we feel in our heart to be right, rather than be motivated by what
our mind decides is expedient.

Thinking and decision-making

We cannot solve our problems with the same thinking
we used when we created them.

—Albert Einstein

Should we make our decisions on how to act or not act on the basis
of thought or on the basis of something deeper than thought? Do we
need to think exhaustively and exhaustingly about every aspect of a perceived problem and its possible solutions in order to come up with the
best solution or is there a short cut? Can we just know the best solution independently of an exhaustive and exhausting thinking process,
or can such a massive train of thought actually derail our best solution?
Perhaps your response to the question posed at the start of the chapter
about your worst decision is that it was made after thinking about a
perceived problem or opportunity in a particular way—excessively and
repetitively. Perhaps this process resulted in your getting stuck in mental
quicksand, where the more you struggled to find a solution, the deeper
you sank into the problem. Perhaps your best decision was made when
you didn't think about your problem or opportunity, and just acted on
the basis of your intuition—a shortcut to a deep and valuable answer.
Perhaps your best decision was made when you allowed yourself enough
time and space to transcend time and space, by focusing on what's happening right here, right now. Perhaps this led to your just knowing a
solution, instead of getting caught up in the worries that thinking about
it can lead to.

Bypassing worries to find a short cut to an optimal decision can be
technically termed "the shower principle." Everyone, or at least everyone
who has regular showers, has probably experienced the paradox of their
answer coming as soon as their question is let go of. Showers are great
places to let go of anything, except the soap! A variant of the shower
principle is when the answer comes to us while we are taking a walk,

going for a run, or enjoying any other time when we are free of the burden of making decisions, and can therefore be more creative about finding an answer, or even enjoying the process, simply by getting out of its way.

There might be a special advantage offered by activities that are physical and not mental, such as having showers or going for runs, because these can help us literally "come to our senses." Our senses are the reality of our immediate bodily experience, rather than the unreality of our imaginings. I had a boss once who was a particularly busy professor of geriatric medicine. His only daily break from worrying about decisions on how to best run a busy geriatric research institute was during his lunchtime run. My erstwhile boss told me that this was when he made his best decisions.

I once had another professor, of cognitive psychology, who actually devised a very complex model that explained what everybody already knows once they stop thinking about it. The model was based on a spreading activation theory of human cognition, which describes how a series of interconnected nodes (information units) constantly talk to each other. When our decision-making process is narrow, our information nodes mainly only communicate with the next node in the thought production line; they form knowledge in-groups. When we relax and allow our decision-making process to spread outward, rather than inward, our mental nodes communicate with lots of other nodes, and an answer therefore often comes from an unexpected source. This could also be called lateral thinking or open-mindedness—or mindfulness. Whatever we call it, if we are in a state of consciousness that's open rather than closed to our opportunities, we will make better decisions and we will make them more restfully, creatively, and enjoyably.

Daniel Goleman outlined a highly useful psychological construct that he termed emotional intelligence.[2] This has contributed toward a new way of looking at intelligence that differs greatly from the traditional idea of it as something that allows us to break mental rocks in a similar way to how a computer does it. Emotional intelligence basically consists of self-awareness, the ability to act (including decision-making actions) on the basis of our self-awareness, empathy (awareness of other selves as not being that different from our selves), and the ability to act well socially on the basis of this empathy. This construct clearly relates to mindfulness, and indeed the great humanistic psychology professors Daniel Goleman and Jon Kabat-Zinn actually made a CD together discussing how a working relationship between emotional intelligence and mindfulness can help us live and work better.[3]

Professor Goleman cites a study in his dialogue with Professor Jon Kabat-Zinn of the decision-making style of extremely successful Californian business entrepreneurs. The results of this study showed that these successful decision-makers tend to make their decisions on the basis of a two-stage process. In the first stage, they accumulate as much relevant information about the full nature of the situation as they can—this could be seen as the awareness phase. In the second stage, they just recognize that they know what to do at a deep level—this could be seen as the intuitive phase. Many of the entrepreneurs said that they frequently made successful decisions that were inconsistent with what their information suggested they should do because they "felt right."

There's a neurophysiological explanation for the importance of our gut instincts and how we can make better decisions if we trust our feelings more than our thoughts. The basal ganglia is a primitive structure in our brain that gives us an ongoing record of our deeper knowledge (perhaps there's even an aspect of us that knows what our minds don't). The basal ganglia isn't connected with our speech centers or our other higher order cognitive processes, but it is connected with that which can know what our mind doesn't: our bodies. Can you think of a situation when the facts seemed to suggest one way of proceeding, but your heart suggested another and you went with your heart—and you were right? The American mindfulness expert Jon Kabat-Zinn has pointed out that in many Asian languages the words for "heart" and "mind" are the same, so mindfulness and a mindful response to decision-making could equally correctly be called heartfulness.

Decision-making and listening

When people talk, listen completely. Most people never listen.
—Ernest Hemingway

There's a little known principle of human physics that states, "The more we talk, the less we listen." It might help us to listen if we realized that what we are actually listening to when we listen to anyone fully and deeply—mindfully—is ourselves, our deep selves. It's only in the stillness of true listening that we really hear anything, that we really learn anything. When we do this, we can make optimal decisions that are based on what is (reality) rather than on what seems to be (perceptions).

Socrates is an ancient Greek philosopher who wasn't formally employed as a workplace consultant, but he enthusiastically advocated the use of philosophical principles to help people work as well as live better. Most people in fifth-century Athens did to Socrates and his working-life wisdom what most people mostly do to offerers of great life and working life truths now: they ignored him. Not everybody ignored Socrates, of course, or we would never have heard of him. The people who didn't ignore him, including Plato, listened to him so intently that this annoyed certain rich and powerful Athenians, so much so that they poisoned him.

According to Socrates, the truth is the ultimate answer to all of our questions, and therefore the only proper basis on which to make decisions. The great problem with our habitual decision-making, according to Socrates, and the cause of many of our problems, is that it's usually based on our idea of truth rather than on the actual truth. Hence Socrates practiced and advocated a system of dialogue as the ideal basis for making decisions. This "Platonic dialogue," or "dialectic," was named after its written recorder and popularizer, not after its inventor, and it begins with the notion that there is truth—there is a right way to act—and this truth doesn't belong to anyone. The active ingredient of the dialectic approach to communication and decision-making is that we need to ask questions that can take us, and the people with whom we are communicating, to the truth. It's the opposite to the adversarial system that's commonly used in government, courts of law, and many other workplaces that have forgotten or never knew Socrates and the power of truth. A vital principle of the dialectic approach to communication-based decision-making, as opposed to the imposing-my-will approach to decision-making, is that we need to start off with the idea that we might be wrong. This simple shift in our usual ego-based mind position can make us free—free to make decisions that will be reasonable, fair, and sustainable.

You can probably think of examples of workplace decision-making that haven't employed dialectic principles. Maybe you had an experience when you or a colleague did something that your boss didn't like, and the boss's response decision involved a telephoned/texted/e-mailed/physically screeched expression of considerable displeasure. Maybe the response decision took another destructive form, such as demotion or exile. Was this response decision an example of the dialectic principle in workplace action? Was it constructive? Was it mindful? How might the boss have acted differently and ultimately more successfully for everybody, not just for the abused or otherwise damaged worker? What if the boss had asked a question, such as, "Why did you do what you did?" What if the boss had started his or her response with the premise that perhaps his or her opinion of events was just an opinion and not the absolute truth? Could there be far better working outcomes in millions of work situations every day, including our own, if all of us simply listened to other people at least occasionally and let go of our rigid ideas about truth as something that's ours and ours alone?

Decision-making and ethics

Fanatics are picturesque; mankind would rather see
gestures than listen to reasons.
—Friedrich Nietzsche

Being mindful means being connected to everything, including other people. Therefore, acting in a reasoning and reasonable way that recognizes our integral connection to others means not making decisions that will hurt them. The first principle of medicine is given in the Hippocratic Oath: "Do no harm." A version of this oath could valuably be taken by people doing any job—dentists, accountants, lawyers, hairdressers, medical researchers, advertisers…. Unfortunately, many decisions made in the professional world are unethical, which simply means harmful.

What causes unethical decisions? Obviously, if we don't give a damn about the welfare of other people—if we are not mindful of our connectedness—we can easily make a workplace decision that we know will cause harm and simply not care about it. An example of this kind of decision-making process is where the CEO of a large company decides to manufacture and market a product, even though they are well aware that it will cause harm. The results of these kinds of decisions can be as varied as the increase in sales of alcohol to young adults due to the manufacture and marketing of products that are particularly appealing to them, or the increase in infection-related infant deaths in Third World countries due to the manufacture and marketing of products that lead to mothers giving their infants these rather than breast milk. When the motivation for our actions is personal profit, we are being mindless and destructive.

Unethical decisions are also made on the basis of ignorance of the outcomes of our actions, as well as on the basis of knowing what the likely consequences will be and then ignoring them. An example of this ignorance would be a farmer selling his livestock without knowing the details of their subsequent treatment, and that subsequent treatment being unethical. Another example would be that of a retailer unknowingly selling a product, or a consumer unknowingly buying a product, that has been produced by people who were treated unethically. We need to be mindful in all aspects of our decision-making, and this may result in our asking questions about the details of the product or service that we are producing, selling, or buying.

Some examples of mindful working decisions

All our final decisions are made in a state of
mind that is not going to last.

—Marcel Proust

Sometimes the most important thing in our lives in general and also in our working lives isn't how mindfully we make a decision, but how mindfully we stick with it. As with many situations, it's often best in our working decision-making to be in the middle of certainty, rather than on the edge of doubt. The decision-making middle-ground lies between rigidly sticking to our decisions that deep down we (and everyone else) know are wrong and capriciously bending in the breeze of popular opinion by changing decisions that deep down we (and everyone else) know are right. We need the courage and the wisdom to recognize when we are going in the wrong direction and to modify our decisions accordingly, just as we need the courage and the wisdom to recognize that we are going in the right direction and to keep going there.

Before Woody Allen was a star comedian and actor in his own right, he was a joke writer for other comedians, including Sid Caesar, who just happened to be large, strong, and at least occasionally ferocious. "I hate your joke!" Sid once fumed at a trembling Woody.

"I'm not married to it!" Woody responded with laudable non-attachment.

This is an example of a time when it's appropriate to change professional direction. There are also times when it isn't, no matter how difficult things are getting. Ultimately, no matter how tough the going is getting, it will only get to be impossible if we are going against the direction that we deeply know is the right one. How then do we know what the right direction is? The more mindful we are, the better the chance we'll have of knowing our true selves and therefore our true direction.

The following are some personal examples of work decisions that some of my family members have had to make and that I have had to make. These are not clear-cut examples of mindful, as opposed to mindless, decision-making, and so they are perhaps useful to people in situations where their way forward isn't fully clear either.

My father's father was once the star center halfback for the South Warrnambool Australian Rules football team. At that time, many players in the prehistoric version of what is now the Australian Football League (AFL)—the Victorian Football League (VFL)—were recruited to play for Melbourne clubs (and the Geelong club) from the country, maybe because all the fresh country air made country boys grow into fast and skillful footballers. Some of the leading VFL clubs tried to recruit my grandfather to play for them, and they successfully recruited a star opponent of his who went on to win the coveted Brownlow Medal for the league's best and fairest player.

My grandfather wanted to move his family to Melbourne and play football at the highest level, of course, but my grandmother didn't want him to. My grandmother thought that my grandfather might get injured and lose his ability to work, which would mean, at least temporarily, losing their livelihood. At that time, people played high-level football for love, and not for love and money. Maybe my grandmother also didn't want her family to leave their life in Warrnambool. Whatever the reason, they stayed. When I found out about this decision (as a child), I was appalled. Why wouldn't you go to play VFL football if you could?

What I didn't realize back then was that sometimes we have to make decisions that are more fundamental and therefore of greater consequence than most. What job should I choose and where should I do it? I don't know whether my grandfather made the right decision or not—only he knew that. But I suspect that if he made his decision mindfully—from a deep place, from a place of silence where he really knew what was important in his and his family's life and values—then he made the right decision, and there would have been no (or very few!) regrets.

My other grandfather, my mother's father, volunteered to fight in World War I, even though he was a strong pacifist. I don't know what led him to make that decision, and he never spoke of his wartime experiences. I suspect that he made his decisions to go to war and to later be silent about it from a place of deep knowledge.

The only decisions that we can at least partly truly know about, on the basis of our own experience rather than on the basis of speculations about other people's experiences, are our own decisions. My own working decisions have included some where I agonized long and hard, and then decided what to do once I stopped agonizing and started listening to the sounds of silence instead, to my deep knowledge of who I am and how I could best express this in a job.

I left my home, family, and friends in Geelong on a freezing pre-dawn morning in the winter of 1988, to fly off to tropical Darwin to teach statistics to nurses and other conscripts, and to become the brand new Northern Territory University's inaugural cognitive psychology lecturer. This was a tough work gig that involved students who sometimes threw paper airplanes at each other rather than listen to my attempts at stand-up statistics; and things were sometimes lonely so far from my previous home. I never regretted the decision to take the job, however, because the decision was made and recognized at a deep place. I ended up doing what I loved, which gave me the strength to keep doing it even when I hated it—or thought I did!

Ten years later, I left my job as a researcher at the Victorian Transcultural Psychiatry Unit at St. Vincent's Hospital/University of Melbourne, to buy and renovate historic houses (via a sojourn in India). Times were often tough in this working holiday from academia, including times such as those spent up a high ladder in the wind, nailing in boards in scary unison with a colleague on an equally high ladder hammering in the other end of the same board; and times spent dismantling (demolishing?) a chimney in an historic house that was donated to my new business by the Australian House Museum, Deakin University. A representative of the university visited the house one day while it was still on the university grounds, saw my learned colleague and me covered in sweat and grime and dust, and remarked, "This is hell!" I never regretted this change of working direction, however, because that decision was also made from a deep place and resulted in my doing what I loved.

Recently my wife and I decided that, despite her being a trained architect and secondary school teacher, her most valuable work would be achieved by staying home and looking after our new baby daughter. We haven't regretted this decision because we made it from a deep place—from love. Not a love of relative poverty, but a love of love!

Some techniques for mindful decision-making at work

It can be useful to be aware of why we are making our decisions before we make them, which means knowing enough about ourselves to know what will really work out well for us and others. It might therefore be useful for us to try to be more and more aware of our deep basis for making decisions, by being more and more aware of what we are really working toward. Is it security, acclaim, fear, or a love of what we are doing and who we are doing it with? We need to decide who we really are and what really works for us, rather than decide who we think we are and what we think works for us. The more mindful we are, the easier it is for us to make decisions based on knowing rather than based on thinking that we know.

When I was so young and innocent that I consistently practiced mindfulness rather than wrote books about it, I was highly impressed by some applied mindfulness. A very long time ago my mother created a mindfulness box, which gave my brother and me a wonderful opportunity to attend to stuff that we needed to in the moment—when we opened the box—such as collecting our lunch money. Every day, we read our daily reminder to be mindful before anybody used the term, because it was written in huge letters on top of the box: Do It Now!

I once had time to play chess, which incidentally is a great way of developing mindfulness as it develops the ability to focus on what we mean to focus on. This is also true of many other activities that have lost popularity in an increasingly simulated world, such as sewing and playing musical instruments. These have been increasingly replaced by much more mindless and disconnected activities, such as watching TV, texting, and playing computer games. There was an adage in chess that

I liked: "A bad plan is better than no plan!" The point of this was that if we do something, then even if we end up doing it wrong or thinking that we are, we still learn something.

To move from chess to another thought sport—advertising—Nike famously employed a mindful message in their "Just do it!" campaign. This campaign was created in the same year that Prozac was, 1988, and demonstrated that a mindful message—to act rather than to think about acting—can be widely and successfully recognized. Nike's "Just do it!" campaign resulted in the company increasing its share of the U.S. sports shoe market from 18 percent to 43 percent between 1988 and 1998. It was apparently based on the last words of convicted murderer Gary Gilmore, who was executed in Utah in 1977. We can spend far too much of our working time meeting, developing, planning, and analyzing rather than doing, so try just doing—and doing it now.

Take-to-work tips for mindful decision-making

- We make our best decisions when we let go of our need to make decisions.
- Just do what comes naturally rather than decide to do what seems unnatural.
- Ultimately, we don't mindfully make decisions about people; we make mindful decisions for people.

Chapter 4

Mindful Leadership at Work

Remember the difference between a boss and a leader:
A boss says, "Go!" A leader says, "Let's go!"

—E.M. Kelly

The Macquarie Dictionary defines a leader as "a guiding or directing head, as of any army, movement, etc."[1] The leadership "etc." is enormous and includes leadership in the community, family, and workplace. A more expansive definition of leadership is offered by Vince Lombardi, the head coach of the Green Bay Packers football team during the 1960s, as well as a leadership expert: "Leadership is based on a spiritual quality: the power to inspire, the power to inspire others to follow." Leadership isn't about telling people what to do; it's about showing them what to do.

No matter how we define leadership, most of us have personally experienced the vastly different effects of good and not-quite-so-good leadership on our workplace happiness and fulfilment. As with many other important life activities, such as breathing and driving, leadership can be performed consciously or unconsciously. It can also be performed selfishly or unselfishly. Mindful leadership means leading ourselves and others consciously and unselfishly, and to do this, it's vital that we know where we are going so that we can help others get to where they are going. And to know where we are going, we need to know where we are. Without full consciousness of our here and now reality, we are leaderless and lost. If we don't know where we are, or who we are, how can we help anyone get anywhere else? Leadership begins at home.

59

Mindless leadership models

*An employee's motivation is a direct result of the sum of
interactions with his or her manager.*
—Bob Nelson

Many leadership models have evolved throughout the adventure of our human history. Some of these leadership models have been extremely successful; others have been extremely destructive. Not surprisingly, these models differ considerably in how closely they follow the principles of mindfulness.

The Renaissance was a fascinating chapter in our human history that involved a magnificent rediscovery of the cultural, artistic, and philosophical light that ancient Greece had given the world about 2,000 years previously. The physical epicenter of the Renaissance was in northern Italy, particularly Florence, which gave us such great figures as the writer Dante Alighieri, the painter Michelangelo, the philosopher Marsilio Ficino, and the just-about-everything Leonardo da Vinci. The Italian Renaissance also gave us a vastly influential leadership manual called *The Prince*.

Niccolò Machiavelli wrote his Machiavellian leadership manual in 1505, and handwritten copies were distributed to princely personages well before it was posthumously published in 1532. *The Prince* was possibly the world's first political philosophy book, and it hugely influenced how princely people in 16th-century Italy ran their family leadership businesses, as well as their acquired leadership businesses. This book still greatly influences our modern world, particularly our political leaders and those of us who are affected by their leadership style (i.e. most of us). Modern business leaders, workplace leaders, and even family leaders frequently demonstrate Machiavellian principles in action, even if they have never read or even heard of Machiavelli's most famous book. The leadership principles and tactics espoused in *The Prince* could be succinctly summarized as "The end justifies the means."

The Prince was targeted at those who particularly needed the specialized self-help that it offered, and its avid early readers included heads of the small states—principalities—that make up modern Italy. It was an amazingly pragmatic work in that it instructed its readers in how to be "free" to lead selfishly by separating their personal morality from their leadership morality. It also offered them practical take-home tips on how to manipulate, trick, and bully their way into power, and keep it. Machiavelli targeted princes who had acquired power more than he targeted those born into it because this was seen then, as well as now, as being a fundamentally more difficult gig. Prior to the emergence of *The Prince*, highly ambitious leaders or potential leaders had to rely on their own unassisted natural talent for manipulation, trickery, coercion, and bullying.

A particularly destructive mindless leadership model was espoused by Adolf Hitler in *Mein Kampf* ("My Struggle"), which he wrote in jail in Germany after he unsuccessfully attempted a political uprising there in 1926. Adolf Hitler wrote *Mein Kampf* with a "friend" and "colleague" (Rudolf Hess), although this wasn't acknowledged when the book was completed and published in 1930. It wasn't specifically written as a leadership manual, unlike *The Prince*, but it had a powerful effect on how a lot of people saw successful leadership, including the people who willingly followed Hitler into World War II.

A primary leadership principle espoused and demonstrated by Hitler as author and mindless leadership role model is the Machiavellian notion that the end justifies the means. If we believe in something strongly enough, such as the perceived interests of the organization that we are leading or aspiring to lead (such as a business or state), then according to mindless leadership models, we are justified in acting in a way that's not necessarily advantageous to other organizations (such as other businesses or states). These leadership malpractices may result in their practitioners ending up totally unable to see a difference between the interests of the organization they represent and their own interests.

An important leadership principle that can be either negative or positive was espoused in *Mein Kampf* and negatively demonstrated in the leadership career of its author: the power of persuasion. This power is based on the recognition that it's easier to manipulate people's emotions than it is to manipulate their reason—to persuade them to do what we want them to do and not necessarily what they want to do. Particularly effective ways of leading people to mindlessness via their emotions are through appeals to their personal greed or by planting the idea in them that they need to respond to a great threat (by following you). The emotions that Hitler manipulated in the German people—and that Napoleon manipulated in the French people, and that Genghis Khan manipulated in the Mongolian people—included pride in their country and leader; fear of various state "enemies," and anger with these same "enemies." "My struggle" soon became "my world's struggle."

The leadership model offered by Machiavelli and other mindless leadership theorists and practitioners is based on selfishness: what's in leadership for me and mine? This selfishness can happen at many levels and usually isn't very successful if the "self" involved is just myself. Usually the self at the heart of essentially heartless leadership models involves some kind of extension of the self in charge (or the self who wants to be in charge) that's inclusive enough to recruit sufficient people to help the power-junkie achieve power. If Adolf Hitler had tried to drum up enough enthusiasm in other people to help him achieve a totally personal power, then he probably would never have achieved it no matter how convincing he was. Hitler was cunning enough, was Machiavellian enough, to know that he needed to appeal to a desire for power that was broader than his own personal ambition. He appealed to the desire of the German people to supercharge an entire country's power. This leadership model can be described as personal power-based leadership.

There have been many famous historical examples of personal power-based leadership practitioners including such successful (if not necessarily truly great) leaders as Genghis Khan, Alexander the Great, Napoleon Bonaparte, and Idi Amin. Although he didn't write a leadership manual, Alexander the Great outlined his view of leadership in a single statement: "I would rather face an army of lions led by a sheep than an army of sheep led by a lion!" Napoleon succinctly noted that "A leader is a dealer in hope." What's common to all these personal power practitioners is fear, both in themselves in the form of a deep insecurity that compelled them to seek a compensating, controlling power, and in the people they "worked with," their followers or victims. The personal power-based leadership style centers on the idea that people need to be controlled, that life needs to be controlled.

The personal power-based leadership model has led to a large number of extreme situations such as wars and other unnatural disasters at an international level, including the massive famines orchestrated by Josef Stalin in the Soviet Union, Mao Zedong in China, and the many modern African leaders who deliberately created food shortages to control their constituents. It has been practiced at a national level by many political leaders who put their own interests above the interests of the people they led.

At a local level, the personal power-based leadership model has resulted in extreme workplace unhappiness, and at all levels mindless leadership makes leadership a burden—rather than an asset—both on those who are led and on those who lead. We are surrounded by the destructive effects of mindless leadership; there are blatant examples of this in the media and in industry, as well as in politics. You might even have had personal experience of mindless leadership in your own workplace, whether your workplace is a multinational corporation or a small suburban beauty salon. Mindless leadership is a massively destructive problem that affects many people's happiness and life fulfilment, but is there an alternative?

Mindful leadership models

We are the ones we have been waiting for.
—June Jordan

It might seem like life is rushing past us so fast these days that we are about to lose the human race, but maybe the answer to many of our most pressing problems, including our working problems, is to slow down rather than to speed up. Why rush to get there when we don't know where we are going? When we are mindless and stressed, we might think that successful leadership means leading people to go even faster than the people we are trying to keep ahead of, but maybe successful leadership really means leading people forward by leading them backwards...to stillness. Maybe if we can lead ourselves and others to this state of subtle but vast opportunity, our potential working paradise is only mindlessly mislaid and not lost.

Two and a half thousand or so years ago, some people thought that life in their modern age was unnecessarily stressful. Some people back then were rushing around mindlessly making and selling stuff that they didn't believe in and not giving a damn about anyone else. And Gautama, the famous Buddha, said way back then that modern people were just rushing, rushing, rushing—from birth to death—without stopping to focus on the blurred bit in between. This was as modern an age as this one is, to the people who were there, and it was brimful of the same modern mindless maladies that we think we've invented.

Two and a half thousand or so years ago some especially great life leaders emerged, in two very different parts of the world, possibly in response to the (then) great modern need to focus modern life's blur. Gautama the Buddha emerged near Varanasi in northern India as the inspirer of the great Buddhist wisdom tradition, which offers us some deeply valuable lessons in good life leadership. The great Socrates/Plato philosophical double act emerged in Athens, Greece, at about the same time. A pressing point that emerged strongly in mindful leadership manuals such as the Buddhist *Dhammapada* and Plato's *Republic* is that we are all leaders of our common destiny and we all lead best when we lead from the front. We can all be Buddhas (fully awake) just as soon as we stop worrying about what we don't have (unreality) and start appreciating what we do have (reality).

About 2,000 years ago, another especially great life leader was born in Bethlehem. Jesus inspired some other vastly life-knowledgeable people to write a life leadership manual over the next couple of hundred years that's still a bestseller: The New Testament. It contains highly valuable leadership tips, including how we can access a vast peace and happiness surplus if we can transcend our petty desire for control at all costs, such as is expressed in our need for greed, and instead act from compassion rather than passion. The leadership model offered in the writings and lives of the great leaders who inspired the world's great wisdom traditions could be described as unity-based leadership, or non-personal power-based leadership.

Some more recent examples of the unity-based leadership model in action include the life and works of inspirational leaders such as Florence Nightingale, who recognized a need to do something highly practical to relieve the suffering of soldiers in the Crimean War, and later to relieve the suffering of people in countries that didn't have adequate sanitation or understanding of its health benefits. Florence Nightingale led by example—from the front—and she was motivated by compassion and a deep knowledge of people's needs. Mother Teresa displayed a similar blend of strength, vision, and compassion in her work for the poor in Calcutta. Another great example of a leader operating from the unity-based leadership model is Mahatma Gandhi, who famously led India to independence by opening people's minds and hearts, and not by the more usual opposing of gross will with gross will. There's also the great modern example of Nelson Mandela, who rose to lead the South African nation by wise example after spending 27 years in a political prison. What then are some of the vital ingredients of mindful, rather than mindless, leadership?

Mindful leadership ingredients

I suppose leadership at one time meant muscles,
but today it means getting along with people.
—Mahatma Gandhi

There are supposedly seven secrets of success,[2] seven pillars of wisdom,[3] and even seven deadly sins. The reason for the proliferation of sets of seven may well be that this is the capacity of most of our working memories—about seven items, plus or minus two.[4] Perhaps unsurprisingly then, there are seven key ingredients to mindful leadership!

1. Courage

Do not follow where the path may lead. Go instead where
there is no path and leave a trail.

—Harold R. McAlindon

If there were a Viking leadership manual, it would probably start with the words, "Die with your arrows in the front!" The Viking leadership manual might also end with these words. This leadership advice might seem rather odd, as well as unmindful, but wait—there's an explanation! The Vikings believed that it was honorable to go down in battle, and that if they fell in battle, they would be transported by suitably lovely and respectful young creatures to their rightful place in Valhalla—paradise. There was, however, a small-print section in the Viking warrior code that stated that to get to Valhalla, one needed to do more than just die in battle; one also needed to die with one's arrows in the front, which means facing the enemy. The metaphor thus encapsulates a key ingredient of mindful leadership: it requires courage (which is not to be confused with aggression).

The great courage that mindfulness requires from us is the courage to face reality, so that we can lead ourselves and others into it. Ultimately, this reality is the reality of who we really are. And at the risk of exceeding the Viking mindfulness metaphor quota, really facing ourselves can make facing an angry and well-armed Viking seem like a walk in the park!

At least one ancient wisdom tradition has listed courage as the first required attribute of anyone who would like to achieve enlightenment. Without courage, we won't get anywhere, and therefore we won't be able to lead others anywhere. We need courage to start a job worth starting and to complete it. Courage allows us to wake up to who we really are and where we are really going, and to help others wake up and get where they're going. Without courage, we would just do what we did yesterday, again and again and again. Without courage, we wouldn't be able to see that there's a better way than the way we've trodden so many times that we are downtrodden. Without courage, we won't even realize that there's a better way.

2. Charisma

A great person attracts great people and
knows how to hold them together.
—Johann Wolfgang von Goethe

The Harvard psychology professor and mindfulness expert Ellen Langer gave an inspiring presentation on mindful leadership at the 2011 ADC Future Summit in Melbourne. In this talk, she simply defined mindfulness as the ability to see subtle differences in things, which means seeing the newness in things. The real job of any leader, according to Ellen Langer, is simply to inspire people to be more mindful. We can be there—living in reality—or we cannot be there—living in unreality—and where we are affects where others are. If we are really there, we will do well in life and in our working life, and enjoy ourselves. If we are not really there (because we are somewhere else), then we will not do well in our life or our working life, and we will not enjoy ourselves. Which life and working life state should we choose? A wise leader can help us to choose, and thereby live and work wisely.

The fundamental quality of a good leader, according to Ellen Langer's ADC Future Summit presentation, is charisma, and charisma comes from seeing the newness in things and inspiring others to see this newness. The former American president Bill Clinton was accused by many people of being many things, but he was widely recognized as having great charisma. It could be said while his charisma made the people with whom he came into contact feel very special, he achieved this result simply by giving them his full attention. If we give people our complete attention, then we are being completely mindful; we are seeing something new and therefore fascinating in them, and they can therefore see something new and fascinating in us.

Ellen Langer mentioned in her talk that leadership can be a particularly challenging issue for women. Scientific studies have shown that if women act according to certain traditional feminine roles, they are often perceived as being weak leaders. Other scientific studies have shown that if women act according to certain non- or neo-traditional feminine roles (such as by imitating a man or somebody's idea of one), they are often perceived as being...less than perfect. However, Ellen Langer also referred to the results of one of her own studies that showed that if a woman simply acts mindfully, she rises above such judgments.

Charisma is the core of the leadership apple. We can be so charismatic just by giving our full attention to what and who we are working with, that people will want to follow our example. An example of great mindful leadership in action that might seem as weird as the Viking leadership example is offered by a sergeant in a B-grade movie that I once watched. This unofficial mindfulness maestro had the charisma to inspire others to follow him into an extremely challenging situation—attacking a well-defended enemy position—by courageously and creatively responding to their situation in a marvelously novel light: "Come on, you bastards! How can you get to heaven if you don't die?" How can we lead ourselves or others to our full potential if we don't let go of what we think we know?

3. Be a conductor, not a controller

To see things in the seed, that is genius.

—Lao Tzu

Great leaders such as Nelson Mandela and Mother Teresa transform the people they lead, and they do this by transforming themselves. Great leaders transform themselves and others by recognizing a potential greatness in them that might otherwise never be discovered. Marva Collins is a great American educator and leader who rose out of poverty and achieved enormous success teaching "unteachable" children from similar backgrounds to her own. She was such a practically successful educator and leader that she was eventually offered the position of U.S. Secretary of Education by Ronald Reagan and again by George Bush Sr. Collins refused on both occasions because her vocation was to teach, not to tell people how to teach. In her inspiring book, *Marva Collins' Way*, Collins described the secret to successful education: help people to discover and believe in their abilities by discovering and believing in their abilities.[5]

There's a well-known saying that "perception is reality." Similar leadership advice is offered by the 4,000-year-old ancient Indian Vedic philosophy: "What we give our attention to grows." What grows is either our harmony or our chaos.

Ellen Langer once conducted an experiment that involved asking one group of musicians to play a piece of classical music as they had played it before, whereas another group was asked to individually introduce a subtle novelty into their performance that nobody else would notice.[6] The music played by both groups of musicians was recorded and evaluated by the musicians themselves and by others. The novel, and therefore mindful, music was rated by both the musicians and others as being better. Interestingly, classical music is played in a group work situation where mindful individualities might seem like de-harmonizers of the collective output, but actually the opposite effect was found. Collective output was better orchestrated when orchestra members mindfully introduced novelties into their music making. Maybe what helps wake up individual members of a group also wakes up the entire group—to its full potential.

A successful leader is like an orchestra conductor regardless of whether he or she is leading a sporting team, a retail outlet, or a pig farm: a successful leader knows whether individual energies are being played out harmoniously or not.

According to the ancient Indian Vedic philosophy, the entire universe is made up of a play of three energy types: rajas (movement), tamas (structure and stability), and sattwa (light). If we are conscious of the balance of these energies playing out, in ourselves and in others, we can orchestrate our lives far better than if we are unconscious of them. If we are aware that we or others are in a state of too much or too little movement or structure or light, we can help balance this state. Great leaders are conscious enough of their own and others' energy balance to successfully orchestrate subtle beneficial changes, just as great jockeys don't just rely on their whips but are sensitive to the energy balance of their horses. They therefore conduct great performances rather than trying to force them.

4. Listen to the signal, not to the noise

Knowledge speaks, but wisdom listens.
—Jimi Hendrix

Being fully mindful means really listening to people, and at work that means both those who work for us, as well as those we work for. If we are fully mindful, then we will naturally really listen to people because we won't be distracted by our ideas about what they are saying. If we can really listen to people, we can find out where they need to be led. It might seem that leadership is all about telling people stuff and not listening to them telling us stuff, but this idea relates to a style of leadership, rather than to actual leadership. Good leaders take people to where they really need to go, not to where they think they want to go or to where we think they should go.

The Wizard of Oz wasn't a great wizard or leader in any ordinary way, and at one level he was a fraud. At a deeper level, though, he was a great leader because he saw the real situation of the people who came to him: a scarecrow who thought he needed a brain, a tin man who thought he needed a heart, a lion who thought he needed courage, and a girl who thought she needed a home. The Wizard of Oz led all of these people out of their delusions by really listening to them, by really listening to the signal of their deep selves that was obscured to everybody else by the noise of their egoic selves. The Wizard of Oz saw that each of his visitors already had what they were looking for, so he could lead them to themselves.

5. Enthusiasm

Example is not the main thing in influencing others. It is the only thing.
—Albert Schweitzer

How can we inspire enthusiasm in others if we don't have it ourselves? How can we be enthusiastic about life if we are not engaged in it, if we are not mindful? If we are fully mindful, we can see people and situations as if for the first time, and therefore fully enjoy the adventures of our life and our working life. If we can see our work situation as if we have never seen it before, then we can see the wonder in it and we can be enthusiastic about it. Children are naturally enthusiastic about life because they are naturally totally engaged with it, totally interested in it, totally mindful. Workers who love their jobs are naturally enthusiastic about their working life because they are totally engaged with it, totally interested in it, totally mindful. People who are enthusiastic about their jobs can naturally lead others and themselves to achieve great things through their work because, like mindfulness, enthusiasm is infectious.

Citizen Kane is considered by many film experts to be one of the greatest films of all time. Like many great achievements, *Citizen Kane* was the result of a lot of hard work, but hard work such as building the great pyramid of Cheops or writing an annual performance review doesn't just happen. We need enthusiasm to inspire hard work. Orson Welles was a 25-year-old "boy genius" when he made *Citizen Kane* in 1941. He was a technically brilliant director, but far more importantly, he was also extremely enthusiastic. Orson Welles described days when he could barely bring himself to turn up at his film studio because he was frozen with self-doubt and just didn't know what to do next, but he turned up for work anyway, even if all he had to offer was his enthusiasm—and it never let him down. The actor Vincent Price was once asked which director he had enjoyed working for the most, and why. The answer was Orson Welles, not for any technical reason but because he gave his actors wonderful things to do! To lead people to wonderful places, we need to experience wonder, and we need to be enthusiastic about life's working potential.

6. Non-judgmental awareness

Be the change you want to see in the world.
—Mahatma Gandhi

Being non-judgmentally aware and being a great leader might seem like things we have to choose between. Actually, being non-judgmentally aware is key to being a great leader. It might seem like leadership by definition involves judgment in that it involves evaluation: we have to judge the performance of those who work for us and even those for whom we work. But must it? Perhaps we are assuming when we evaluate others, professionally and personally, that people consciously decide to do stuff that disappoints us professionally and personally. But do they? If we have the empathy to see things from the other person's perspective, even those we are leading in some way, might we realize that what they're doing actually makes perfect sense to them, and therefore potentially to us?

A key aspect of mindfulness is being open to new experiences and the adventure of the present moment—including to the magnificent possibility that we are wrong and that somebody else is right! Many apparent truths of life have proven to be false once they were investigated by someone mindful enough to value the dynamic novelty of their own experience above unquestioned facts. If Galileo's team leader or Leonardo da Vinci's team leader had been asked for an appraisal of their performance, they might have failed to see the value in their employee's new way of looking at their genius-defining problems! Good leaders recognize opportunities for perspective shifts, rather than remaining inappropriately loyal to particular ways of doing or seeing or evaluating things.

Being non-judgmentally aware means allowing ourselves a more creative view of apparent mistakes—both ours and other people's—and therefore being less likely to generate mistake "labels." This ability allows for wonderful serendipities, such as the discovery that a certain bread mold wasn't really an annoying laboratory mistake but a life-saving drug called penicillin. This ability allows for important discoveries, such as that the sun doesn't circle the Earth like most people thought; the Earth circles the sun. We can even see evolution as an interactively intelligent process and not just as a series of random mistakes. If we are mindful, we can be non-judgmentally aware enough to see mistakes as opportunities for positive change, and inspire the people for whom and with whom we work to transform themselves from mistake-ridden ugly ducklings into mistake-free (or at least mistake-resistant!) swans.

7. Unity

Me, we.

—Muhammad Ali

Mindless leadership often results in a clash of individual wills between people who all want to be leaders rather than be led. It's a paradox that the people who want to lead often don't make good leaders. This phenomenon can happen at a national level, such as in the power plays of our political leaders, and it can also happen at a local level, such as in the power plays of our own workplace leaders. The motivation for leadership is vital. If we are leading for ourselves because perceived control makes us feel important or because we enjoy lording it over others, then we will eventually end up alone and unsatisfied—no matter how many people we are leading in that same direction. If we are leading for others, because we can help them get where they're going, then we will end up in a state of unity and deep satisfaction—no matter how few people we are leading in that same direction.

Great leaders recognize that people other than themselves have talents, and that other people don't necessarily just perform their functions to help them showcase their own talents. Great leaders recognize that energy works best when it flows, and that energy doesn't flow very well at all when it's stuck in the quicksand of our ideas about who it belongs to. A free working energy flow is equivalent to the free economic energy flow that free trade allows, and the claims of personal credit or accusations of personal blame obstruct this flow in the same way that economic protectionism obstructs economic energy flow. Great leaders don't care about whose great idea gets up, just that it gets up. This is epitomized by the Japanese leadership model's emphasis on identifying collective solutions rather than individual blame for collective problems. Great leadership doesn't mean a separation of leaders and led; it means recognition of the unity of great working relationships.

A parable of mindful leadership

Once upon a time there was a new CEO of a large airline somewhere in the world who decided that the business should be more successful, soon. Once upon another time, there was a new CEO of a small clothing manufacturing business somewhere in the world who decided that the business could be more successful, when the time was right. Maybe the new airline CEO started out in his leadership role with a strong motivation to improve his organization's productivity to justify his extremely high starting salary, which many of his employees resented. Maybe the new airline CEO started out in his leadership role with an urgent desire to justify the faith of the people who gave him his job. Maybe the new clothing manufacturer CEO started out in her leadership role as the inheritor of a family business. Maybe the new clothing manufacturer CEO started out in her new leadership role with a motivation to produce a great product and to share its potential benefits with both her workers and customers.

Whatever the reason for their starting out in their leadership roles, each of these new leaders soon had to work out what success is. Does success mean selling more plane tickets or clothes, decreasing costs, or both? Is real success more than, and more sustainable than, increased profits?

The new CEO of the large airline soon identified areas of "inefficiency" in his attempts to increase the airline's profits. This was a similar process to the worldwide identification of "inefficiencies" by workplace experts in the 1980s and '90s.This process led to implementation of the lucrative workplace restructuring principle of simply making your customers line up longer for whatever you're offering them, so that you don't need to employ as many staff. Airline jobs were therefore shed in the interests of improving "efficiency," and services were reduced for the same reason. Other "efficiencies" were soon added, such as excessive penalties for customers' slightly overweight luggage and minor lateness. The airline's profits went up, for a while, but then they sank to lower than their previous levels because of the long arm of the law of working karma: people don't like being treated badly.

The new CEO of a clothing manufacturing business identified ways that her company's product could be differentiated from the competing cheap imports, such as by improving its quality and also its uniqueness and relevance to its intended market. This was despite being advised by an expensive "expert" consultant that the best way to increase profits was to cut production costs and retail prices by shedding staff. This CEO was mindful enough to listen to her workers, customers, and potential customers, as well as to her consultants, and then to courageously and creatively respond to their input and also to her deep intuition. The clothing company went on to profitably produce a product that people were happy to produce and to buy. The clothing manufacturing CEO also had the novel idea of combining positive principles of capitalism and communism: she offered her staff shares in the company. There was soon a mutual increase in the unity and fulfilment of the CEO and of her staff. The company was successful in both economic and human terms.

A technique for developing mindful leadership at work

We all learn better by doing things than we learn by being told things. There's a group activity that's taught in the Lucca Leadership Program in Italy and in other places that shows people that things work out better when we are all going in the same direction. This technique/game also demonstrates that good leaders harmonize many potentially separate activities into one activity by introducing what we can describe here as a simple three R leadership literacy program:

1. Realize the task's optimal outcome.
2. Recognize whether or not the people doing the task are each and all working toward the optimal outcome.
3. Respond to any non-optimal changes in direction that may creep in during a task or series of tasks.

To practice this leadership training technique, or play this game, just find or make a pole that's long enough for every member of the working group to hang onto with at least one hand. Then simply invite the group to lower the pole to the ground. This might sound simple, and it is if people work together, but usually what happens is that people get tense, try too hard, try to do the task individually, or compensate for others not doing what they think they should be doing, and the pole goes up, not down! Usually groups only succeed in lowering their pole when a leader or leaders emerge who direct the group's efforts so that they pull together, rather than push apart. Pole orchestration practically proves to people that working harmony works a lot better than does individual chaos.

Take-to-work tips for mindful leadership

- Mindful leadership means leading naturally and unselfishly.
- What we try to control controls us.
- Great leadership begins with our ability to lead ourselves— to who we and others ultimately are and to where we and others are ultimately going.
- Great leadership means working for others, including those whom we are leading. Oscar Wilde's time spent in prison doing hard labor allowed him the great insight: "Whatever happens to another happens to oneself."
- We don't have to be right to be great leaders; we just need to know what right is.
- Great leadership means leading us all to a better place.

Chapter 5

Mindful Relationships at Work

I don't like to commit myself about heaven and hell;
you see, I have friends in both places.

—*Mark Twain*

What makes a great working relationship great? Between us, there's an answer. This doesn't just mean that we are more likely to find a solution to our working challenges if we work with other people than if we work against them. It also means that none of us individually has the answer, especially when we think we do. The only solutions that will really work out for us, and others, are those that don't belong to any of us. Really workable solutions arise only in the silent space that none of us owns, that exists silently between us. When we each get off our righteous working platform, we can be free to see what the best outcome really is and not just what we think it is or would like it to be. The best working relationship is the same as the best any other kind of relationship: no relationship.

The idea that the best form of anything can be no form of it might sound strange, but this is actually our natural life state, which mindfulness can help us to reach. Life is richest when it isn't limited by the small print of conditions or ideas, when it's just life. We live best when we just live, and we work best when we just work, and this means working in such a natural state of flow with our fellow workers that we aren't even aware of having a relationship with them because we are flowing together.

A key part of all of our lives is our relationships with other people, and this is particularly true of our working lives. How well we work with other people—whether they are technically above us or below us or on a par with us in our working pecking order—will have a huge effect on how happy, fulfilled, and productive we and our working partners will be. In this chapter, we will explore how we can work mindfully and therefore productively, happily, and harmoniously with all of the people we work with—our employees, employers, and fellow working travelers.

Albert Einstein was a clerk in a patents office in Switzerland who managed to find time to find time. Einstein's general and special theories of relativity explain time, space, and matter, and our place in the whole show. The basic idea of relativity is that nothing means anything by itself, and therefore nothing exists independently. We can only measure movement by measuring the movement of one object relative to another. If there aren't two of anything, there can be no movement. It's the same with relationships. If we are mindful enough to transcend our ideas about how good we are and how good what we are doing is, then we can be free to do as well as we can in working harmony with the people with whom we are flowing so seamlessly that we can all work absolutely optimally, not relatively poorly. We can only work optimally when we work with others optimally. And we can only do this when we get off our ideas platform, where we are waiting for our next train of thought to take us to our desired working destination—more money, more security, more prestige, more of the relative me in whatever form. No matter how shiny our working part is, it's only a part not a whole.

Jean-Paul Sartre, the French existentialist philosopher who famously said, "Hell is other people," obviously knew what it's like to live and work with difficult people! We can now link some of his key working theories with some from another great if possibly previously unrecognized working relationships theorist, Albert Einstein. Sartre might well not have meant that hell is having other people around. He might have meant that hell is having relationships with other people. Maybe the opposite of hell is being so connected and happy with other people that we don't see them as being "other" people. Maybe working existential relativity means not having working relationships, not having ideas about a pecking order, and this lets us go with our mutual work flow so smoothly that nobody gets pecked.

Mindless working relationship models

Assumptions are the termites of relationships.
—Henry Winkler

Have you ever worked with, for, or over someone, and it was like working in hell? Have you ever worked with or for or over someone and it was the complete opposite of hell? What was the difference? There are plenty of examples of how we can work mindlessly, and therefore destructively, with others that can help us to see the active ingredients of unworkable work situations and how we can work our way out of them and not into them.

You might have thought of some of your own examples of mindless and destructive working relationships, and if you have, you might be able to think of how their mindlessness manifested, and with what results. As Thomas the Gospel writer and workplace theorist observed in the New Testament, it's only by finding the light of our consciousness that we can enlighten our darkness. If you can't think of an example of a mindless working relationship, lucky you! Here are some examples for you from literature, reality, and some other public domain working-relationships instruction sources to help illustrate what doesn't have to be.

The American playwright Eugene O'Neill once claimed that there is only one type of happy family but that every unhappy family is unhappy in its own way. He was probably well qualified to make his claim because he wrote a (posthumously premiered) play about his own family called *Long Day's Journey Into Night*. In this same courageously close-to-home spirit, we can look closely at mindless working relationships and usefully divide them into types, depending on whether they involve our bosses, our underlings, or our working equivalents. Further distinctions can be made using some of the wonderful examples of difficult-to-relate-to types of people provided by psychologist Andrew Fuller in his book *Tricky People.*[1]

Mindless relationships with bosses

It might seem like the most blatantly mindless examples of our working relationships are those that involve bosses, and if you thought of a personal example of a non-mindful working relationship, this may well have been its type. An interesting thing about power and its relationship to our happiness and harmony though is that, like mermaids, what it looks like depends on how far we are away from it. From great distances, lonely sailors once mistook relatively physically unlovely sea creatures such as dugongs for relatively lovely sea creatures such as mermaids. It's the same with power.

From a distance, power can look ravishingly irresistible, like something we want more and even more of, but up close, it can look like something we don't need. Andrew Fuller mentions bullies and tyrants as an important class of tricky people, and these are perhaps especially prevalent among mindless bosses. Basically, if someone constantly wants us to do something we don't want to do, or if we constantly want others to do what they don't want to do, then there is bullying going on and possibly even tyranny. This sort of mindless working relationship often has unfortunate results on people's happiness, productivity, and even health. Bullies and tyrants are driven by a need to have power over others, and this need can manifest in different ways, including full-frontal standover tactics and sly, malicious manipulation.

Working relationships with people who mindlessly hold strong opinions about anything can be difficult, but working with people whose strong opinions are about their own worth can be particularly challenging. People with excessively high self-esteem often end up as bullies or even tyrants, because they tend to want others to share their high opinion of themselves and get angry if they don't. A psychological theory, or at least a popular idea of a psychological theory, stated that bullies are people with very low self-esteem who are trying to compensate for this by being bullies. They aren't. Bullies are people with high self-esteem who want to zealously spread their opinions about themselves to people who will listen to them voluntarily as well as people who won't.

Another general category of tricky person, described by Andrew Fuller, who is often a mindless boss, is the high and mighty. Again, this mindless type is likely to include people who are above us in our working pecking order, or who think they are, but this isn't always the case. Self-importance and its potentially destructive effects on others is only a state of mind, or mindlessness, after all. You might be able to think of an example of someone who was technically lower on your working pecking order than you, but who had an extremely high opinion of him or herself. Maybe you had to help them puff up their inflated mindless idea of themselves by performing some kind of subtle penance before they would let you do something you needed to do—such as pass their reception desk to start work! High and mighty types are basically driven by their belief that they are better than others. This mindlessness set is a potential problem for other people because high and mighties usually aren't content to just bask in their superiority theoretically; they also want to actively demonstrate it to others. High and mighties have a strong sense of a better and therefore separate ego, and they can be mindlessly destructive as a result.

Mindless relationships with the bossed

It might seem like the easiest person to have a good working relationship with is somebody who works on a lower branch of our working pecking order—our supposed underlings—but, as with many ideas, this one might not be as true as it seems. The apparently weak can have a destructive tyranny over the apparently strong. You might be able to think of an example from your own workplace or another life situation where you have been dominated by someone who is supposedly weaker or at least smaller than you. (Parents of small children or adolescents might find this particularly easy!)

There is a nice example of the strange complexities of power relationships in the movie *Fiddler on the Roof*, where a beggar asks passersby for alms. A passing businessman tells the beggar that he can't give him any money because he hasn't made much of it that day. The beggar haughtily, but logically, demands to know why he should suffer because somebody else has a bad day at work! I had a similarly strangely complicated power relationship with supposedly more powerless people than me when I was a relatively impoverished visitor to India, by visitors' standards of course. I ended up taking tuk-tuks (auto rickshaws) up the mountain to my early morning Vipassana mindfulness meditation sessions in downtown Dharamkot, because that was a cheaper option than walking past the early morning beggars with whom I had developed a cordial but expensive relationship!

I have also had similar strangely complex power relationships with my university students who, according to someone's ideas at least, I was supposed to be in charge of. They threw paper airplanes at each other during more than one of our classes in preference to listening to my vital statistical insights, which I eventually put into book form for those who missed out.[2] I have also had strangely complex power relationships with my house-renovating employees, one of whom once told me that I would be in serious trouble indeed if she broke a nail!

We can be precariously perched above someone else in our working pecking order even if we are gainfully employed as a dishwasher third class, as George Orwell once was in Paris before he wrote a bestselling book about being "down and out in Paris and London." It may not, however, be an unmitigated joy to be technically on a higher working plane than someone else is—such as a dishwasher third class if they are a dishwasher fourth class, or a President if they are a Vice President—if at least one of us isn't mindful enough to work with awareness and acceptance of our working relationship.

Power perceptions are often complex. To what extent people's perceptions are mindlessly ego-based rather than mindfully trans-ego-based can be an important decider of how well we work with others and with ourselves. Relationship perceptions are often dangerously distorted by our seeing ourselves as superior or inferior to other people, and such difficulties generally start with criticism and with judgments. It might be difficult at first to not criticize others—no matter where they are placed, or misplaced, on our working pecking order—but this is a vital step toward our working freedom. Can a destructively mindless working relationship manifest when we don't see ourselves as better or worse than other people because we don't judge them and therefore don't criticize them? Can we be fully happy and fulfilled at work, or anywhere else, if we think that someone else (including the boss or bossed) is responsible for our happiness and fulfilment? The best place to start not criticizing or judging is with ourselves, because what we do to ourselves we do to others.

Andrew Fuller describes three types of tricky people who provide good examples of people who are often involved in mindless bossed working relationships. Most of us probably know at least one avoider, and most of us have probably worked with, or against, at least one. Avoiders can be lazy or distracted or otherwise lacking in a working awareness of their job description. Avoiders often emphatically agree with us about the task that we want them to do; it will be done beautifully, punctually, magnificently—but ultimately by somebody else.

Then there are the blamers. It wasn't their fault; it was somebody else's fault—their fellow workers, ours, their parents, their karmas. The whiners are the workplace lions led by workplace donkeys (their bosses) and they can do everything better than anybody else can but, for some reason that none of us fully understands, don't. Whiners are working life critics whose only purpose seems to be to act as superchargers to already irrationally negatively charged minds. The common mindless common denominator with avoiders, blamers, and whiners is an unreasonable avoidance and a criticism of responsibility

Mindless relationships with our working equivalents

And then there are the working relationships that can cause us the most angst of all if they play out mindlessly: working with those who share our perch in the working pecking order. A potential problem of working with those who are technically no more likely to peck us than we are to peck them is that sometimes some equals want to be less equal than others.

This is a common playing-out of our habitual working nature, and it's the basic reason why communism doesn't work, even though it was basically devised to help working life work better for workers. Andrew Fuller mentions competitors as a category of tricky people who can cause other people more bother than they need, and this type of tricky person is particularly tricky when we are working with them. Competitors are driven by the notion that there isn't enough of something—money, prestige, work—to go around. This mindlessness set can be an adult manifestation of the childish thinking that often results in such seemingly senseless accusations as "You gave her/him/it one more chocolate than me!"

Extreme workplace competitors can be described by the non-technical term backstabbers. This type of mindless workplace relationship is destructive because competitors see those against whom they are competing as being so separate from them—even if they are working on the same project and for the same company—that they are enemies rather than fellow working travelers.

The mindless working model: some common elements

What links all manifestations of the mindless working model is that ultimately we find it extremely hard to work constructively with others when we are working only for ourselves, or rather for our idea of ourselves. People who can't connect their working parts into a working whole are living and working in a state of mindlessness because they are not fully aware that their humanity extends to the next workstation as well as a lot further. The results of non-awareness of the others with whom we share our workstations and planet can be spectacularly destructive.

There are many possible examples of the spectacularly destructive results that come from working mindlessly with others, and one I will always remember is that of a professional tag-team wrestler whom I once barracked against with my brother as (very young) TV wrestling fans. One member of the extremely villainous and successful tag team once simply refused to tag his equally successful and villainous partner who was in trouble. Despite the beseeching of his workmate, who was literally being stomped on by his adversary, the villainous wrestler simply downed his wrestling tools and just observed—perhaps mindfully but perhaps also inappropriately. This illustrates just what can happen when we care only about our own welfare and don't see ourselves as part of a work or working planet team.

Mindful working relationship models

Oh, the comfort, the inexpressible comfort of feeling safe with a person, having neither to weigh thoughts nor measure words, but pouring them all right out, just as they are, chaff and grain together; certain that a faithful hand will take and sift them, keep what is worth keeping, and then with the breath of kindness blow the rest away.

—Dinah Craik

Fortunately, there are plenty of examples of mindful working relationship models that we can emulate. Many of the wonderful examples of mindful and constructive working relationships are also wonderful examples of symbiotically successful unions popularly described as strange bedfellows. Sometimes we are forced by our life or working circumstances to be fully aware of the true nature of our working situation and of the person with whom we are sharing it. Sometimes this is because we are mindful enough to be creatively inspired by the possibilities that a successful relationship with a very different but very complementary workmate can offer. Sometimes we form these successful working relationships simply because there's no other choice and we are mindful enough to recognize that. Sometimes our only workable choice is to win or lose, and we can't just stay safe and miserable in our working mediocrity any longer. Sometimes we are forced to choose between mindlessly ignoring our situation and mindfully accepting it. This choice can be the vital first step that can ultimately take us anywhere—to the moon and over it.

The Defiant Ones is a wonderful movie made in 1958, starring Sidney Poitier and Tony Curtis. The characters played by Poitier and Curtis perfectly demonstrate the potentially profound benefits of working harmoniously and productively with someone else when circumstances force us together. Most of our working relationships don't start off with perfect match compatibility checks, such as those used in computer dating, so our working circumstances often force us to work with people with whom we might not immediately think we are compatible.

Poitier and Curtis's characters experience an extreme form of workplace "bondage": they are literally chained together, as part of a chain gang in the Deep South of the United States. Our working relationships often involve similar bondage when we enter and conduct them mindlessly, but usually such bondage is subtle, metaphorical, or imaginary. To make things even more interesting, as well as educational, Tony Curtis plays a young, angry, racist white, while Sidney Poitier plays a young, articulate black. The plot of *The Defiant Ones* soon thickens, and our duo is given the opportunity to escape from their chain gang—together. They run hectically through fields—avoiding attack dogs and bullets—and they run together. Eventually both escaped convicts realize that no matter how differently they see each other, and how differently they think each other is, they can only escape their mutually hostile fate if they work on escaping it together. These characters are perhaps uniquely fortunate to be in such a diabolical workstation, because it forces them to realize that, at least sometimes, we can run together or fall alone.

A more positive and less fictional example of workers finding more together than apart is the song-writing partnership of the Beatles' John Lennon and Paul McCartney. John Lennon formed a promising skiffle group called the Quarry Men in Liverpool in 1957. At that time, it wasn't immediately obvious to the entire planet, or even to the Liverpudlian bit of it, or even to the pre-Beatles' (1960) friends, that this group was going to be big.

Paul McCartney was a slightly younger Liverpudlian neighbor of John Lennon's, and even in those pre-famous days, he was widely recognized as being prodigiously talented. McCartney was a highly proficient player of many instruments, including the piano and guitar, and the 17-year-old John Lennon considered inviting him to join his pre-Beatles. The decision to ask McCartney to join him was actually a complex one, because if any of us asks a very talented person to join our work gang—of any kind—we can risk reducing our perceived potential glory.

Lennon was mindful enough to be aware of the positive as well as negative possibilities of working with another genius, and his response to this awareness resulted in his inviting McCartney to join him—forging a success that was far greater than the success of any part of the whole working relationship would have been.

Decisions to turn working parts into greater working wholes have to be made in the same way that all decisions are made: now. It isn't possible to make decisions based on what will look good in the future. Deciding to do what we know is best, and not what we think is best, takes an enormous amount of courage because it means we are working without an ego net. This is ultimately a mindful act because it's only when we are mindful that we can be fully aware of our working potential and its integral link with the working potential of others. When we combine with others so successfully that we don't need individual credit, we transcend our individual working limitations.

A common mindful denominator of constructive working relationships is that they involve working effectively with other people. We are all connected. We can only really work well with others when we are mindful of who they really are, and we can only form this optimal working partnership if we are mindful of who we really are.

Working together

Whatever happens to another happens to oneself, and if you want an inscription to read at dawn and at nighttime and for pleasure and for pain, write up on the wall of your house in letters for the sun to gild and the moon to silver "Whatever happens to another happens to oneself."

—Oscar Wilde

Whether our work involves doing hard labor in Reading Prison, as Oscar Wilde once did, or whether it involves our being professionally witty at dinner parties and theatrical opening nights, as Oscar Wilde also once did, or whether it involves something somewhere in between (which most of our work does), how well we do it with others has enormously important consequences. The consequences of not working well with others can include psychological and physical illness, as well as more common forms of unnecessary misery such as not wanting to get out of bed in the morning.

You might be working in a workplace similar to many of mine, where the people doing one job often resent the people doing other jobs. When I was a postgraduate student, working late at night at college on my PhD thesis, the security guards resented students, especially nocturnal ones, and we resented them. We didn't understand each other; we thought we made work for each other. We missed the point that other people don't get in the way of our work; rather, they give it meaning. If we had been more mindful we would have realized that we needed each other—that we were part of a larger system that included us both. Mindfulness expands our working relationships until we are all on the same side and realize it. Mindlessness contracts our relationships until we are just me.

There are many scientific studies that objectively demonstrate that mindfulness helps our working relationships,[3] as well as helps our workplace performance[4] and workplace well-being.[5] Mindfulness can greatly help us at work by opening us up to the adventure of finding out who we really are and, even more adventurously, being comfortable with who we really are. The great ancient workplace relationships expert Gautama the Buddha pointed out that we need others to achieve full awareness, or enlightenment. Working well with others can put us in the express lane on the freeway to enlightenment, because it gives us a crash-less course in knowing ourselves through knowing others and knowing how we best relate to others. Increased knowledge of who we really are will help us to find out who others really are, and help us to work with them optimally as a result.

Being married is a great opportunity to get to know ourselves through knowing somebody else; so is working with someone else. In fact, sometimes working with others can be even more challenging, and even more rewarding, than living with them can be. We might think that we can work happily with anyone, except the person with whom we are actually working, just as we might think that we can live happily with anyone, except the person with whom we are actually living.

Deepak Chopra reminds us well of the mindlessness of such thinking: However good or bad you feel about your relationship, the person who you are with at this moment is the "right" person, because she or he is the mirror of who you are inside.

Our modern progress is causing our happiness levels to regress, and this is at least partly due to an increasing disconnectedness in our lives and in our working lives. This disconnection might also be caused by a reduction in our sense of knowing what we are supposed to be doing, including what we are supposed to be doing at work, and why we are doing it. A hundred years ago, it was easy for us to know who we are; we could simply and truthfully say something as wonderfully obvious as "I'm a mule skinner!" or "I'm a princess!" Nowadays, we have a lot more things to say but also a lot less certainty about who is saying it and why. Perhaps an offshoot of our increasingly fuzzy logic about who and why we are—in a world of ever-shortening fashion cycles—is that it's getting harder for us to work with a sense of common purpose. How then can we work with others more mindfully, effectively, creatively, and enjoyably? How can we regain our naturally mindful sense of connectedness with the people with whom we work and live?

Proximity

A good way to connect with our fellow workers is to actually see them—up close—at least occasionally. These days, far more of us are working from home and in other non-traditional working environments, which is perhaps a less than perfectly understood consequence of our technical, or at least technological, progress. This progress has brought us closer to other people in that it's now physically and financially much easier to drop in on someone in Reykjavik (if we don't live in Iceland) than it used to be, but this progress has also distanced us from other people, in that it's now psychologically and socially harder to drop in on our immediate neighbors than it used to be. A hundred thousand or so years ago, we were ridiculously primitive—we didn't have mobile phones or apps or the Internet—but presumably we also didn't have much trouble forming a meaningful bond with the people in the cave next door, or in forming meaningful working relationships with the people with whom we were hunting or gathering.

Empathy

A powerful way of establishing connectedness with our work colleagues is to share something important with them, including something as practical as empathy. This really just means acknowledging that we are all on the same side of our work team, if not on the same side of the planet. Scientific studies have shown that empathy is generally decreasing, or at least decreasing in the bits of the world that do these studies. A University of Michigan study of approximately 14,000 American college students showed that empathy, in this sample at least, has declined about 40 percent in the last 20 to 30 years.[6] Suggested reasons for this decline include exposure to levels of video violence that numb young people to the pain of others, and social media, which encourages people to have online friends rather than friends that others can see too.

If we are mindful of others we will naturally realize our connection with them and we will also recognize that we all have a common goal—especially those of us who are officially working together, or are supposed to be. The senior management of many workplaces take their staff off on development days or weekends and fill their heads with ways to improve the organization's bottom line, whether the bottom line is biscuits produced, houses sold, brains filled up with academic theories, bottoms on stadium seats, or whatever. Could it be simpler, cheaper, and ultimately far more effective to just give workers a crash-less course in empathy? And could this professional human development automatically create the team spirit (unity) that workplace consultants often force feed their workers? This workplace battery hen–style mental pellet feeding often comes from the Unity or Bust working relationships style—and often doesn't survive the trip home from the staff development session.

A course in empathy could valuably start off with a reminder of what's known as "the golden rule." Variants of this appear in all of the world's great philosophies and religions, including "Do unto others as you would have others do unto you" (Christianity), "Never impose on others what you would not choose for yourself" (Confucius), and "None of you [truly] believes unless he wishes for his brother what he wishes for himself" (Islam). It can be a hell of a lot easier inside or outside any philosophical or religious belief system to do mutually good things unto others if we don't think of them as "others."

How mindfulness can help us to work together

An integral part of the success of any organization, as well as an integral part of the success of the people who work in the organization, is the quality of its component working relationships. This is true whether our organization is a benign behemoth such as a large city council with thousands of employees, or a small fish-and-chip shop with just one or two employees. When we plan how to run our organization better, we might not immediately consider how improving its working relationships will improve its financial and human profitability. However, the most valuable resource of any organization is its human heart, and how the individual humans that make up any organization interact with each other and others is vital to its overall optimal performance. A working organization is like any other organization, including a family. If we considered ways to improve how well our family works without considering the relationships between family members, then we would be unlikely to come up with any real or lasting improvement. It's the same with our workplaces: we can't separate the whole from the bits that make up the whole.

What's it like to work with someone successfully? What's success? Does success mean making more money, or does it mean being happier and more fulfilled in our work? Success means both of these things and more, and being mindful can help us to achieve real success by helping us to work more productively and also more happily, together. We all know what it's like to work with someone else successfully. We all know what it's like to work with someone else unsuccessfully. We all know which of these options works best for everyone.

When we are completely mindful, we can do everything that we do optimally—naturally, enjoyably, productively—even work...especially work. When we are mindful, we are in a state where it's natural for us to relate to others as well as we can, and therefore work with others as well as we can.

Some working relationship examples

A good thing about my having wide-ranging professional experience is that it gives me the opportunity to use a wide range of personal working examples, like an actor who has learned something useful about a whole story from their experience of many parts. A good thing about a mindful approach to work is that it gives us a greater perspective than the small-world view of "me and my problems." This can help us to see that our working roles are like all of our life roles—just roles. We will get deep life satisfaction from playing them well, but ultimately we will do our work optimally and enjoy it fully when we don't over-identify with our roles and mistake them for our ultimate reality.

I once took an extended working holiday from work as a lecturer to renovate historic houses. I had an idea that there would be a considerable and welcome difference between my being an academic and being a "house artist," as I saw myself. Like most stories we tell ourselves, this one turned out to be less real than it seemed. My first on-the-new-job lesson in applied mindfulness was that I needed to listen very carefully to the people who were constantly telling me things because I soon learned that in the school of tangible hard knocks, rather than the university of metaphorical hard knocks, it only takes as long as the fall from a ladder to accumulate enough empirical evidence to be convinced that something has gone wrong. I soon learned that most of my ideas about renovating houses and about the people whom I employed to help me work on them were fantasy rather than fantastic. I soon learned that to get a great working result, we need great working relationships, even if we think we are going it alone.

Another mindful lesson that I learned as a renovator was that I needed to be fully aware of the deep reality of the houses that I was working on. When I was completely aware of the house that I was working on, and what it needed from me to help it become the best that it could be, I forgot my ideas about how it should turn out or could turn out. A famous sculptor once said that sculpting is easy; you just take away everything from what you're sculpting that doesn't look right, until it looks right! I grew to understand what he meant. The process of fully connecting with the houses soon expanded into a process of fully connecting with the people who worked on them with me. When this process worked so well that the results weren't individual-ego based, but collective-insight based, then the end product as well as the journey benefited enormously. It felt like we were all part of a common energy field, doing the same dance.

There were challenging moments for me when I played the working part of a house renovator, such as the moment when I stepped down from working on a higher level, metaphorically and literally, onto a ladder that wasn't there—a ladder that someone had mindlessly removed. This gave me a wonderful opportunity to choose between mindless hostility and mindful acceptance and forgiveness! There were also magically mindful moments, such as the one when I realized that I needed a small cutting brush to finish a painting job, and one magically materialized from the hand of someone who was also focused on the same specific need. And there were moments when my work colleagues and I were all at the pub for lunch on a Friday arguing without malice about diverging house-improving ideas, which made me realize that my colleagues felt listened to enough to really care about what they were saying.

A plumber working on a particularly historic house (shipped to Australia from Singapore in 1852 as an early "kit house") suggested once that we cut viewing panels into the new plasterboard to reveal the historic wallpaper over timber slats. We did, and the Council's historical expert whom I invited to that house's unveiling was highly impressed with that feature and even more impressed with the story of working unity that inspired it.

Some techniques for developing mindful working relationships

Coming together is a beginning; keeping together is progress; working together is success.

—Henry Ford

There are some valuable and simple techniques that can help us to work more mindfully. Unlike the seven ingredients of mindful leadership, the seven mindful working principles, and the seven deadly sins, there are only six of these. You are welcome to think up your own seventh technique!

1. Working openly

Mindfulness naturally opens our mind-created closed doors, and this gives us open access to our full range of life and working life opportunities, including our working relationship opportunities. When we are mindful, we are fully aware and fully able to focus our awareness. When we are mindful, we have an open mind and an open heart, and therefore we are fully connected to other people, and the business and life opportunities that they continually offer us. Modern medical knowledge suggests that our minds are located in our physical brain, and ancient medical knowledge suggested that our minds are located in our physical heart, but when we fully open our minds into mindfulness, they transcend the limitations of locality, and this expanded awareness will help us to connect deeply and productively with others

I once participated in a postgraduate psychology training program in West Timor, Indonesia, before the principles that underlie mindfulness were commonly described as mindfulness. The training program included playing a game where we explored some barriers that often get in the way of us working effectively with people whom we see as being different to us. A potential perceived difference between people was deliberately created in this game by having each of us learn one of two sets of cultural values and beliefs. We were then presented with a situation where we needed to transcend our perceived differences to work well together and achieve an optimal result. We weren't told, however, that we needed to work together to get the ultimate result!

My group learned cultural values and beliefs that could be described as "imperial." We learned that our culture was the world's most advanced and economic expansion was desirable—inevitable—and required us to expand our business operations into previously untapped resource bases (virgin rainforests). The other group learned cultural values and beliefs that could be described as "indigenous." They learned that people are a more valuable commodity than any economic one, and that economic ends do not justify inhuman means of achieving such ends. We were then put together without being told anything about each other's "cultures."

We imperialists were told that the people we would soon meet were the primitive custodians of valuable rainforest resources that we needed, and our mission was simply to get these resources however we could. This turned out to be a wonderful opportunity to choose between a mindful and a mindless response to a novel work situation. None of us chose a mindful response to our working opportunity. None of us simply listened to members of the other group with an open mind and heart, or considered who they really were and what they really wanted. We therefore missed our opportunity to best work together to achieve our mutual best outcomes. We instead tried to work out how we could get what we wanted from the other group by trying to think of solutions that were doomed—because they came from the closed systems of our existing worldview, even though we had only learned it five minutes ago! We were irritated by the strange and apparently meaningless behavior of the other group of people, who five minutes before had been our friends!

The other group members stood very close to us and made peculiar sounds, which interfered with my group's frantic and narrow solution-driven thinking processes. If my group members and I had been mindful, we would have realized that the other group members were trying to establish human contact with us before discussing business. Instead, we saw their behavior as being random, strange, and annoying—different to our own. Eventually one of us suggested, only half-jokingly, that we simply take our desired resources by force! Being mindfully open means being open to new possibilities, such as the realization that people who are apparently hopelessly different to us are actually an integral working part of our combined greater whole. This example of a choice between a mindful and a mindless response to a situation involved people from arbitrary and simulated different cultures, but the destructiveness of closing our minds and hearts to others can also happen with people at the next workstation.

2. Working networks

Networking is a fashionable term these days, but what does it actually mean? Networking might sound like something that high-powered business executives do for fun or profit, and it is at one level, but as with most things that sound good and that people usually don't understand, there's actually a deeper and more valuable meaning. Networking essentially just means forming an interrelated system where each part of the system is integrally related to each other part of it, and each part of the network benefits from and contributes to the entire interrelated system. We are all part of a network, whether we have heard of networking or not, and this network is called humanity. It might not seem like it sometimes, but we all feed each other information and we all need each other—sometimes in obvious ways, sometimes in subtle ways. Perhaps the modern version of Dean Martin singing in the 1960s about everybody loving somebody sometimes could now be "everybody networks with somebody, sometimes."

The human brain is a gigantic network. There are about a hundred billion cells in each of our brains—maybe a few less in the ones whose owners like too much wine or stress—and all hundred billion of these cells are physically, as well as functionally, connected with each other by cell endings (dendrites) and by chemicals. When we think a thought or stub our toe, this phenomenon affects all hundred billion or so of our brain cells. Incidentally, when I first studied psychology more than 30 years ago, we were taught that we have about four billion brain cells, so either we've become a lot smarter since then or a brain cell counter has been working hard.

We work best with other people when we realize that what we do affects them, no matter how large our working organization is. This realization doesn't come from a thinking process or from a networking propaganda poster placed on our staff notice board. This awareness of our functional connectivity—our working shared hard drive—comes automatically when we are mindful. What then do we need to do or not do to realize that what we do affects what everybody else in our organization does? As with most things worth doing, we need to start our mindful connectivity process where we are—right here, right now—with the person whom we are with right here, right now.

Mindful connectedness in the workplace starts the same way that any other form of working mindfulness does: now. Working mindfulness begins with this keystroke, or sushi slice, or word vocalized. With being fully aware of it—feeling it, hearing it, seeing it. Once we are fully mindful in our small and immediate activities, once we have filled in our little picture, then we will automatically be aware of our big networked picture: who does what in our organization and how we can best help to fill in the gaps. If we mindfully look after our immediate reality pennies (cents, senses), then our working network pounds (dollars, sentience) will look after themselves.

3. Working communication

There are two basic types of workplace interaction: social and task related. There actually isn't a clear distinction between these types, and what underlies good communication—unity—can't be absolutely compartmentalized. Social interactions can include activities that take place outside work, or outside activities that we might normally think of as work, and these are important in developing good working relationships. We can usefully encourage a breaking down of the barriers between working and non-working levels of relationship in our work activities.

Communication, like most things, can be mindful or it can be mindless. Mindful communication offers deep information exchange because it offers more than just what's immediately obvious on the surface. Mindless communication offers shallow information because it only offers the bare bones, the surface message, and not the real message that often underlies it. Scientific studies have shown that we get far more information from the non-verbal content of our interactions, such as body language, facial expressions, and voice pitch, than we do from the verbal content.[7]

The way that we communicate with the people with whom we work will greatly affect how well we work with them. A face-to-face discussion is obviously potentially the best form of communication because this allows us the richness of seeing the other person's body language as well as hearing the tone of their voice and inputting their actual words. A phone conversation doesn't allow us to see the person with whom we are communicating and the visual nuances of their expression are lost. E-mail and texting only allow us to give and receive the actual word content of communication, and texts usually only allow us a short and often cryptic version of this. There are many more ways for our communication to go wrong if we communicate at a lower level, or if we communicate mindlessly—by not really listening to people—at any level. Obviously, it will be more important in some situations than in others to use higher level forms of communication, and despite the proliferation of working and other relationships being terminated or commenced via text messages and computer screens, this can be a dangerously mindless practice.

The mindful communication bottom line is listening. If we really listen to people, this helps them to tell us what we both need to find out together. If we really listen to people, then we won't waste time working on what we think they want from us, but will know what they really want from us. As an experiment in practical workplace relations—our workplace relations—try really listening to someone at your workplace whom you habitually don't really listen to, and see what you both learn.

4. Trust in work and at work

We can't have a good relationship of any kind with someone we don't trust—especially with ourselves—and this phenomenon is especially true of our working relationships. Trust is based on respect, and respect is based on honesty. When we are mindful, we are honest because we are aware of and accept what is, warts and all. Honesty might not seem fashionable or glamorous, especially in a world teeming with individuals, but honesty is the keystone to good working relationships and therefore good work. People will naturally respect us, and naturally trust us, when we are honest. Ultimately, a respectable and trustworthy organization is one that's made up of respectable and honest individual team players, such as us. When we trust our workplace and our fellow workers, we will experiment, we will create, we will help each other experiment and create, and we will value diversity of opinion. The opposite to a trusting and trusted workplace is a fearing and feared one, where no one experiments, where no one helps others, and where diversity is feared. It's our choice whether we respond to the circumstances of our lives and our working lives mindlessly or mindfully, and if the suffering buck stops with us then things have worked out well.

5. Working from the heart

A great working relationship is just like any other great relationship: essentially we are in it for love and not just for money. Our loving relationships might seem limited to those people we are seriously close to, or want to be, but they are actually universal and are what links us to the universal. According to both Eastern and Western wisdom traditions, love is the glue that joins the universe. (Maybe it's also the glue that links the universe's wisdom traditions.) Love is essential to our well-being, happiness, and productivity, and this includes our working life. But love isn't what it's often presented as being by the mass mindlessness media: something that can wake us up in the night pining for someone we lost or never had. That's romantic love, or infatuation, or obsession. Real love isn't hot and consuming and sleep disturbing, despite what songs such as Elvis Presley's "Burning Love" and INXS's "Burn for You" suggest. Real love is actually temperate; it expands us, and it helps rather than hinders our actions, including our working actions.

A working definition of love is that it's simply the experience of our natural connectedness. One of love's many positive spin-offs is that it motivates us to do stuff, and it's our best motivation to do stuff. If we are motivated to go to work each day by necessity—such as the necessity of making enough money to support us and our family's lifestyle—is that going to be better for us and our family, as well as the people we work with and for, than if we are motivated by love of what we are doing and who we are doing it with and for? We are going to be happier in our jobs and in our lives, and also more productive, if we love what we do. This includes loving what we are paid to do.

We all naturally love life and we can all naturally love our working lives if we can let go of what's stopping us. How? A great place to start loving what we do is to really open our hearts to and appreciate the people we work with—and this doesn't mean starting a string of office romances! If love remains a word that you would rather not apply to anyone you work with or for, then try mindfully connecting with your natural kindness, connectedness, or open-heartedness.

So how do we increase our working connectedness IQ? How can we intelligently inject so much connectedness into what we do and who we do it with that we would do it for free if we had to, as well as for freedom? We need to mindfully focus and expand on our connectedness, where it is, and where we are, by examining our attitudes to the people we work with and for. If we wait for other people to open their heart to their job and to us before we reciprocate, then we might be waiting a very long time for an improvement in our working circumstances! We need to work on ourselves before we can work successfully on anything else, and the best place to start this process is by going straight to the heart of the working matter and opening our own heart—to whatever flies or crawls or slithers in or out of it. Don't worry! When everything challenging has finished crawling into it or out of it, what's left will be real.

6. Dialectic dialogues

The Platonic dialectic communication method was described in Chapter 3, and this can be a powerful way of improving all of our relationships, including our working relationships. Employing the dialectic communication method in our working relationships just means starting out with the realization that there is truth, and that this isn't necessarily my truth. Once we are genuinely looking for truth, we can look for it with others, rather than in spite of them. This process is the opposite of the adversarial system that's generally used in workplaces, and also in many other situations where people are often more interested in imposing their individual will than in working together to find a solution that will benefit everybody. Between us there's an answer.

Take-to-work tips for mindful working relationships

- No matter who our working relationship is with, it can be our greatest opportunity to learn vital lessons about the connectedness of our working parts.
- Work works best if we work with others so seamlessly that it doesn't seem like work.
- We don't need to conduct office romances to work with others in a state of co-operation and love!

Chapter 6

Mindful Creativity at Work

When you ask creative people how they did something, they feel a little guilty because they didn't really do it; they just saw something.
—Steve Jobs

Creativity can be enormously profitable in all areas of our lives, including our working lives, because it gives us the power to do more than we think we can. Creativity can create infinite opportunities for us to do anything and everything, because it allows us to break out of our ruts. We will do any job better and also more enjoyably, even if it's one not traditionally thought of as "creative," if we can tap into our natural creativity.

We are all naturally creative, whether we think we are or not, just as we are all naturally mindful, whether we think we are or not. The reason for this is that creativity and mindfulness have a common source: consciousness. All we need to do to be more creative is all we need to do to become more mindful: let go of what's stopping us—our thoughts, such as the ones that tell us that we aren't mindful or aren't creative or aren't anything worth being. Once we let go of our thoughts about what we are, we can create a brave new reality of what we really are: fully creative, mindful, happy, and productive.

If you're lucky enough to have ready access to a very young human, or even a very young non-human, try to observe them playing creatively, which is what they do most of the time. Very young humans and non-humans are naturally mindful because they naturally see the wonder and newness of things, even if they have experienced these same things many times before.

They recognize that we can never enter the flowing river of life in the same place twice; every experience is new. The very young are far too innocently wise to come up with life-weary ideas such as "Oh, damn it all! I'm sick and tired of playing with this same old ball that we play with every day, in the same old way, in the same old park. Let's go to the opera instead!"

Once we are in that mindlessness set, it doesn't matter whether we go to the opera or stay at home because we won't fully appreciate either. Being creative makes life and working life fun because when we are mindful we can creatively explore possibilities, make mistakes, enjoy ourselves, and pack up and try again tomorrow if things don't work out the way we thought they should.

There's a seed funding program in Silicon Valley that recognizes the enormous commercial potential of creativity. It's called 500 Startups, and it funds young people with creative computer ideas from all around the world so that they can go with the natural flow of their ideas, for as long and as far as they can, and enjoy the intellectual journey as well as the intellectual property. Beneficiaries of this creative funding program include a young man with a simple idea for a mobile phone app that makes it possible to virtually attend house inspections without having to leave your own house, and a young woman with a simple idea for an app that improves mobile phone photo quality. The backers of the 500 Startups' program realize that very few of their funded ideas will ever be commercially successful, but they have a broad enough vision to happily experience about 495 apparent failures in the pursuit of some big commercial and creative successes.

Creativity makes more sense when we are mindful enough to be aware of big pictures, including big working pictures, as well as individual bits of them. Pope Julius II creatively seed funded Michelangelo's painting of the Sistine Chapel ceiling, which allowed Michelangelo to creatively paint it. Life is a big picture as well as an infinite series of small ones, and creativity is what links our lives with their big source. Creative serendipity is a vital element of the evolutionary process: recognizing, allowing, and capitalizing on key successful events, such as a giraffe or CEO sticking their neck out and tasting new and useful opportunities. These creative variations can improve not just species but also business survival opportunities. The creative evolutionary process allows creative systems such as our planet, organization, or body to make a series of in-spired "mistakes," and then to implement something wonderfully useful that reveals itself in these "mistakes," such as a longer giraffe neck or a more expansive business plan.

Seeing big pictures helps to give people, organizations, and species the courage to be creative. What would our natural big picture look like if all, rather than just most, early model giraffes thought, "I simply refuse to stick my neck right out. I'll just stick it out far enough to comfortably reach the leaves on the trees that I can get to easily." What would our big medical picture look like if Alexander Fleming and Howard Florey, as well as everyone else, couldn't see the value of penicillin? What would our big picture of our planet and beyond look like if Neil Armstrong and his backers had been content to stay at home and watch science fiction movies about people landing on the moon and beyond? What would our big human compassion picture look like if Florence Nightingale and Mother Teresa hadn't creatively recognized that human suffering can be reduced if other humans care enough to work creatively and effectively toward solutions?

The current global reductions to medical funding by many govern-ments in response to economic and political challenges are the opposite of acts of courageous creativity, and will have the opposite of the de-sired economic and political benefits. What if Queen Isabella of Castile and others had restricted world discovery funding to those projects that they saw as successfully safe because they involved doing pretty much the same thing as what others had already done? Creativity gives us the wonderful human adventure of being apparently ignominiously wrong many times in order to be magnificently right some times, and this is what allows quantum leaps forward in our personal, working, and spe-cies lives.

Creativity isn't the ability to create something out of nothing—not even magicians can do that. Instead, it is the ability to create a mindset that's free to see new connections between what we have and what we can have.

Work is a wonderful opportunity to be creative, to be mindful, and to recognize and live this vital creative connection. Without creativity, we would just go through our working life motions and emotions without realizing the huge potential that work offers us to create rather than just to react. Mindfulness can help us to work more creatively, and working more creatively can help us to work and live better and more enjoyably.

What is creativity and can we create it?

Psychology describes creativity as a type of intelligence, whereas broader descriptions of human behavior, such as religious, spiritual, and philosophical systems, describe intelligence as a type of creativity. Fundamentally, it is an important human attribute that relates to a universal creative principle.

Psychology has many ways of dividing intelligence into types. A division that goes way back to British psychologist Charles Spearman's early work on intelligence divides it into firstly a general "G" factor, and secondly into particular intelligences that are usually further divided into performance abilities such as number and pattern recognition skills, and verbal abilities which include general knowledge.[1] General intelligence can be described non-technically and reasonably accurately as mental computational ability, and even more non-technically (and perhaps even more accurately) as mental horsepower. Some recent developments of psychological intelligence theories include a growing recognition that intelligence takes place in a context: we use it to help us do stuff, such as work, so intelligence is increasingly seen as a problem-solving ability. Intelligence is therefore a useful thing to have in our working tool kit, whether we work as a brain surgeon, plumber, or shop assistant, because it helps us to do stuff well no matter what we are doing.

Intelligence is much broader (and more useful), however, than just the ability to do addition in our head or remember facts (and fictions). Emotional intelligence was described in Chapter 3 as something that helps us to work well, and to work well with others, because it helps us to see what we and others need. Mindfulness improves our emotional intelligence because it helps us to be aware and accepting, and therefore aware and accepting of others, and therefore connected with them in a way that works well for them, us, and our mutual work.

Developments in psychological theories of intelligence include a division of it that includes creative intelligence.[2] Our convergent intelligence is our ability to be logical, to converge on solutions by a process of reducing and reducing until we end up with nothing but an answer. An example of convergent intelligence is deducing the answer to a puzzle, such as the relationship between time and space or the behavior of our friends. Divergent intelligence is our ability to creatively solve problems, or even to creatively transcend problems, by diverging further and further from our starting point until we might even end up a very long way away from it. An example of divergent intelligence is starting with the puzzle of the relationship between time and space, or the behavior of our friends, and ending with a theory that links all of them. A well-known example of a divergent intelligence test is "How many uses can you think of for a brick?" Dropping it on the toe of the person giving us the test will score us a point for divergent intelligence, but it might also inspire them to give us some personality tests as well!

Another psychological approach to creativity uses the concept of spreading activation, and examines how this process works in our brains in ways that are more or less creativity friendly. Human brains are made up of about 100 billion brain cells (give or take a few) and each of these is connected to the others. When we think, there is a spread of activation of related thoughts and this process can happen in different ways: sequentially, one neural, cognitive, and emotional step at a time; and laterally, many simultaneous neural, cognitive, and emotional steps at a time. Lateral spread of activation relates to Edward de Bono's "lateral thinking" model and tends to result in more creative breakthroughs than does the sequential style because it opens up many possibilities simultaneously by opening up many and more divergent neural connections.[3] Creatively high-functioning people tend to see more connections between events, people, and outcomes than do less creatively high-functioning people.

Our spread of activation style relates to our neurophysiological arousal level, and we tend to be most creative when we are optimally aroused, which can be described technically as the Yerkes-Dodson Law, and not quite so technically as the Goldilocks and the three bears principle: not too arousal hot, not too arousal cold, but just right.[4] Being mindful has a balancing effect on our brain's spread of activation style and arousal level, so that when we are mindful, we don't need to worry about our brain mechanics; we can just go with the natural flow of where we are going a lot more easily and reliably.

There are older and deeper ways of looking at creativity (and at everything else) than through the eye, or the I, of the science of psychology. Religious, spiritual, and philosophical wisdom traditions don't give us explicit theories about creativity as a type of intelligence that we can scientifically test, if we are so inclined, but they do give us a deep feel for what creativity is, in us and in our universe.

There are many creation stories in many religions, spiritual traditions, and philosophies, and also in mythology. Interestingly, these creation stories are often strikingly similar. In the very ancient Egyptian mythology/cosmology/religion that produced the teachings of Hermes Trismegistus, the god of wisdom and learning, there is a story of creation that describes a world of matter emerging from a creative un-manifest that is very similar to that given in the Bible—in Genesis in the Old Testament, and also in the New Testament: "In the beginning was the Word, and the Word was with God, and the Word was God." (John 1:1)

One of the many interesting things about creativity, as well as creations, is that the same process creates big things and small things. J.R.R. Tolkien called the human creative process sub-creation—creations by the created, big and small. We could even see apparently deliberate untruths, as well as works of fiction, as acts of creation because they make something new out of something old.

Shakespeare gave us vital clues about lots of things worth being clued up on, including creativity: "Assume a virtue, if you think you have it not." (*Twelfth Night*) The perhaps better-known modern version of this is "Fake it 'til you make it!"

The creative working part of these creative wholes is that if we wait for the answer, or the "right" job to do, or the "right" way to do it, then we might wait a long time. Perhaps we don't learn our great truths, including our working truths, or even remember them. Perhaps we create them and perhaps our creativity is our most essential human attribute.

Can mindfulness improve our creative intelligence and even our creativity, in general and in our work? And if it can, how?

How creativity can work at work

Creativity allows us to naturally and easily see working solutions because it allows us to see our big pictures well enough to identify gaps in them and ways that these gaps can be filled. The big picture creative approach has been described as systems thinking, which might sound complicated and like something that is only likely to benefit us if we work in jobs such as computer or health systems design, but it's actually a natural way of looking at our inner and outer working environments.[5] The active ingredient of this increasingly influential approach to solving our working problems is the recognition that workplaces and what they work on form systems, connected wholes rather than isolated individual parts. Once we can recognize working wholes, we can recognize the vital connections between them and identify any gaps or opportunities for improving the system.

Systems thinking can allow us to make quantum leaps in the way we work by allowing us to think more broadly and comprehensively, and therefore better understand what we are doing and who we are doing it with—just like mindfulness. Donella Meadows describes systems thinking in *Leverage Points: Places to intervene in a system.*[6] This article offers valuable insights into the nature of systems and how knowing about them can help us to work more creatively and productively.

Meadows gives some examples of "great, big, unstated assumptions" that can have huge effects on our lives and working lives, including the assumption that the Earth is flat, and that economic growth is desirable and necessary. An important aspect of creativity in the workplace is the ongoing ability to not think as others have thought before us, but to think truthfully and originally, no matter what the short-term consequences. Here are a couple of other aspects of systems change described in Donella Meadows' article, and some resulting links to working creativity.

Systems are changed by visionary people constantly pointing out anomalies and failures in old [and unhelpful] paradigms, particularly in places of public visibility and power. An example of a constant creative vision that still hasn't flourished into a widely used alternative and improved working reality is the Australian-Austrian engineer Ralph Sarich's creative orbital engine breakthrough in the early 1970s. This development was based on the recognition that the piston-driven internal combustion engine was, and is, a very long way away indeed from being the most efficient way of powering a motor car. In response to this, Ralph Sarich developed a new and optimal orbital option. But the overwhelming problem facing this potentially revolutionary development was that there were, and are, deeply entrenched commercial and psychological investments in doing things the way they've been done for a long time, whether or not they are being done the best way. Sometimes the most important aspect of workplace creativity is constancy (and diplomacy!) in persisting with a breakthrough that we know to be good, even if it seems as if nobody else shares our knowledge.

The higher the level of system change attempted, the more people resist it. Examples of this principle include religious and civil visionaries who were obstructed. There are many examples of creative workplace visionaries, such as Galileo and his creative astronomical research-based belief that the Earth revolves around the sun rather than the other way around. These visionaries have to constantly look around obstructive people who only see the bits of the total revolving and evolving system that they want to see. Sometimes the most important aspect of workplace creativity is courage.

Workplace creativity can lead to fundamental improvements in how things are done—paradigm shifts. An ancient military example might not be the first place you would look for a mindfully and creatively positive paradigm-changing example, particularly one that's highly relevant to a modern workplace, but the example of Alexander the Great and the Gordian Knot is marvelously timeless. There was a prophecy in ancient Greece that whoever could unravel the impossibly complicated Gordian Knot would one day conquer the world. Alexander the Great was a talented young Macedonian CEO of a well-funded and well-run fledgling world conquest business. He was asked if he would like to try his luck unravelling the Gordian Knot, which tethered a wagon to a stake. Alexander took on the challenge, looked at the problem for a moment or two, then dramatically pulled out his sword and sliced through the knot with a single sweep. Alexander creatively transcended his workplace problem by introducing a paradigm shift, rather than wrestling with it on its own terms, and in so doing creatively freed himself and others from thinking and therefore acting in a particular and particularly fruitless way. The Gordian Knot is a mythic metaphor for our minds: we can't defeat what we can't transcend.

A more modern example of workplace creativity is provided by Steve Jobs. He helped to make apples even more popular than Sir Isaac Newton did when he was inspired to describe gravity by one of them falling on him, or Johnny Appleseed did when he introduced apple trees to many parts of the United States. Steve Jobs was the co-founder and CEO of Apple Inc. and his business acumen combined with his creativity led to him taking Apple from near bankruptcy to record profitability, while overseeing the development of such modern marvels as the icon-based computer operating system and the "iFamily" of iTunes, iPods, iPhones, iMacs, and iPads. Steve Jobs shared Alexander the Great's ability to see things in a new and better way.

Mindfulness and creativity—how and why

The first step in the creative process is for us to be conscious enough—mindful enough—to recognize our creativity. There is compelling evidence that mindfulness helps to improve and restore a wide range of our human capacities, such as our ability to heal, learn, relate well to others, and work more effectively. There is also growing evidence that mindfulness improves our creativity.

Creativity and mindfulness are closely linked; to be creative, we need to be mindful (and heartful) of the newness and unique beauty of things. To put this another way, when we are creative, we naturally see newness and unique beauty. Being jaded by our life and our work is the opposite of being creative, and this unnatural state can lead to our unnecessarily missing out on our greatest life and working life opportunities. Because being mindful means being fully aware and fully connected, if we are mindful we will be fully aware of our opportunities, including those that we become aware of through really listening to other people. This doesn't mean that being creative involves listening to people so well that we can remember and then steal their ideas! Mindfulness allows us to get close enough to situations and for people to be creatively inspired by them—to live and work in the same creative space as others. Creativity connects.

If creativity is our natural state, as suggested throughout this chapter and in many other places, then what is it that stops us from being more creative and more creatively successful? What stops us from being mindfully creative? The same things that can cause us to lose our natural mindfulness can also cause us to lose our natural creativity and, at a general level, these unnecessary impediments arise when we trade in our natural childlike awareness and acceptance and appreciation of reality for a mindless adult make-believe. When we are not mindful, our "maturing" can just be an abandonment of our natural wonder and creativity in the name of being "responsible." We can actually end up increasingly deluded by the sensory impressions of life and our thoughts about it, and increasingly less creatively connected to life itself.

Mindlessness results in a particular type of thinking that is not creative because it is conceptual and time bound, which is the opposite of the state that allows us to be non-conceptual, immediate, and insightful. Our genuine reality, rather than the reality impersonated by our fractious thoughts about it, allows us to know without going through an exhaustive and exhausting mental process.

An ape might type the collected works of Shakespeare perfectly by chance if it had enough time, and in much the same way we might create some working successes when we don't have deep access to our deep-life creative force, but we can be consistently creative and creatively successful when we know what the hard-working random ape doesn't know: what success looks like. Creativity connects us with our deep insightful knowledge of what our goals look like, which can take us to them even if we don't think we know the way. It's easy to recognize a way once we've recognized a destination.

Problems, including work problems, can be divided into those for which we can arrive at an answer by a series of incremental steps, such as how to design a dam that holds water, and those that require specific insight, such as identifying the best place to put the dam, or how to construct one in difficult and unique circumstances. This principle is true and helpful to know whether you are an engineer, a concrete mixer, a secretary, or a public relations consultant, or whether you are doing any type of work that offers you the opportunity to at least occasionally turn a working situation into a life-developing and fulfilling one by seeing something more than the problem by being creatively insightful.

Mindfulness can help us to remember our natural creativity by helping us to forget what gets in its way: the mental junk that obscures the creative clarity of our true working purpose. This mental junk-piling is caused by our mind's fear of not having enough, including a fear of not having enough thoughts! When we lose our focus, we see clutter rather than clarity, and therefore we end up with a head full of second-hand thoughts. Being mindful helps to restore or enhance our natural creativity because it allows us to think thoughts that are shiny and new and not have to live second-hand, second-rate lives and work in second-hand, second-rate jobs. When we are mindful, we switch off our mental au-topilot that only allows us to fly through and sometimes into problems, rather than creatively rise above them. Problems are old; solutions are new.

Mindfulness has been described in the scientific literature as result-ing in a thinking process (or even a non-thinking process) that "does not get hung up on ideas or memories" but instead "just observes every-thing as if it was occurring for the first time."[7] This is the key to working mindfully and creatively, and will allow us to reclaim our natural state of optimal productivity and happiness by allowing us to swap what isn't (our ideas about our lives and work) for what is (right here, right now reality). We can't be mindful or creative in the past or future.

Our habitual way of thinking—in circles—leads to the accumulation of mental junkyards of unfiled and unwanted ideas about doing stuff, rather than just the simple and clear ability to do stuff. We can trust our ability to creatively wing it, whatever it is that we are working on. An important problem with the mental filing system approach to learning from our experience is that mental files soon get too heavy to fit into even the biggest head and retrieval can be slow, annoying, and the op-posite of creative: "Ah yes, I can easily build you that bridge or slice you that sushi you ordered—but did I file that knowledge under 'B' for bridge or 'S' for sushi or 'E' for easy?"

According to the same Friedrich Nietzsche who once said that what doesn't destroy us makes us stronger, our mental accumulation of secondhand thoughts results in our getting stuck in a mental his-tory and inhibits our creation of the new.[8] We therefore need to learn or re-learn how to forget. Our personal history is our stagnant knowl-edge, and our creative thinking capacity can be seen as our living and flowing knowledge that naturally flows around and over obstacles. If we are not mindful, our creative flow can be dammed and damned by mind-concreting questions such as "Where do I start?"—whether we are stuck in the starting blocks of designing a bridge or slicing some sushi or convincing some people that they need what we are selling them.

Mindfulness effectively reduces the influence of our past on our present actions, and it has been described as resulting in a "beginner's mind" or "bare attention."[9] This means thinking that is innocent of such miasmic mental machinations as those that produce complex reasons why things that actually are aren't, and why things that actually aren't are.

There hasn't been much scientific research done so far on the relationship between creativity and mindfulness, but a recent scientific study conducted by a Dutch and an American researcher found that individuals with greater mindful awareness are better able to solve insight problems, which require us to overcome our secondhand thinking patterns derived from prior experience.[10] More work needs to be done on revealing the exact mechanisms that link mindfulness and creativity, but the authors of this study suggest that mindfulness frees our minds from its concepts—our ideas about what is—and helps us to be aware of the results of our non-verbal processes such as intuition, which are used to creatively re-structure problems. An example of this process is converting mountains to mole hills.

Mindfulness may be the best natural antidote that we have for our creative malaises, our periods of non-creative inertia that imprison us in our ideas of our past. Once we wake up to freedom from our mental histories, we can be more creative than we dreamed possible.

Working creatively with other people

When we are fully mindful, we are fully conscious, and this means fully alive and fully creative. When we are fully conscious, we can consciously decide what we will do and who we will do it with, rather than just drift through life on autopilot. When we are fully conscious, we are fully aware of ourselves, and therefore fully aware of others, and our vital links with them. When we are fully conscious, we are free to do things in a new way and not just do them in the same way that we always do them. When we are fully conscious, we will not meet Einstein's working definition of insanity: doing the same thing and expecting a different result.

When we are fully conscious, we are fully aware of and fully appreciative of novelty, including the ever-replenishing novelty of the people with whom we are working. When we are fully conscious, we realize that the relationship with our coworker is brand new, whether we have been working with them for an hour or a decade, because what we are doing with them right now is happening right now and for the first time.

Perhaps we've been discussing with a workmate how we can best expand our camping equipment sales business in an age when people increasingly want to stay at home and camp on their computers. Maybe our workmate is telling us the same old stuff, as we see it—more advertising, cheaper prices, work harder. Maybe they're telling us the same old stuff because we are only half listening to them, only half mindful, only half alive, and only half alive to our opportunities. Maybe once we wake up to the novelty and the excitement of life and working life as it is, we can see things differently and hear things as if for the first time. Maybe the best way forward in our camping equipment sales example is to combine our current business interest—the great outdoors—with our apparent business obstacle, and include waterproof laptops in our camping package deals! This particular idea might be too wet to float, but it illustrates that once we are mindful enough to create new ways of thinking, we are not stuck in the mental rut of what we did and said yesterday.

To use an unexpectedly mindless metaphor for the value of creativity, there's more than one way to skin a cat. How can we create a working paradigm shift if we ask questions in the same mindset that our current answers are framed in, whether we are a professional cat skinner or a nuclear physicist? Einstein made a quantum leap in the understanding of the universe and our place in it by seeing physics in a new way. He asked himself an intriguing question: what would our universe look like if he was riding a beam of light through it? From this creative new perspective, Einstein saw answers that no one had seen before. He might have stayed in his patents office in Switzerland if he hadn't been able to expand his working circumstances by working effectively with others, and this meant sharing his creative enthusiasm with them. When we see newness and new opportunities, we naturally develop and spread enthusiasm, and without enthusiasm we can't do much at all. Enthusiasm is even more infectious than lethargy or fear, so to expand our working world, we need to see the newness of it—we need to be mindful.

Without mindfulness and its creative enthusiasm potential, our working world will be as flat as Christopher Columbus's once was when he persuaded other people to help him find a new world, or at least a new way of looking at an old one. We can all share the adventure of working creatively with others if we go beyond just mindlessly repeating our usual motions and emotions, and embrace the possibility of real change. We can find a new working world by helping others to find it. And as the great cartoonist and working philosopher Michael Leunig once pointed out, we don't find meaning; we offer it.

Some mindfully creative working examples

So just how does mindful creativity work at work? There are plenty of examples of people who officially work creatively, such as authors, alchemists (who created gold from lead), artists, filmmakers, and florists, but there are also plenty of examples of people working in jobs that have an important but less visible creative component. There are even more examples of people working in jobs who could do it far more successfully, and happily, if they did it more creatively.

A wonderful example of someone working creatively (officially) that demonstrates how creativity can transcend boundaries, including working boundaries, is that of the humorous science fiction writer Douglas Adams. In his five-part trilogy that started with *The Hitchhiker's Guide to the Galaxy*, Adams creatively demonstrated the point—by parodying it—that many of us spend most of our lives (and most of our working lives) stuck in a mindless quest for answers. Adams creatively showed us that our real answer is to go beyond answers, by giving us a completely arbitrary one that a supercomputer with a super-analysis capacity spent eons devising by narrowing down possibilities (the opposite to creativity). The answer that the supercomputer in *The Hitchhiker's Guide to the Galaxy* came up with was, famously, "42," which is about as helpful as it sounds.

The next book in *The Hitchhiker's Guide to the Galaxy* trilogy demonstrated the extremely practical wisdom that the question is more important than the answer. The question linked to the answer to the ultimate nature of life, the universe, and everything (42) was calculated by an even larger computer (the planet Earth), which eventually came up with the question "What do you get when you multiply 6 by 7?" This is also about as helpful as it sounds. We get confused by trying to think of answers, rather than by mindfully and creatively transcending them.

We can also be mindfully creative in jobs that don't seem creative, but that actually are (or could be!) more creative than they seem. These more-creative-than-they-seem jobs include just about any that you can think up. To begin at the beginning, alphabetically, being called a "creative accountant" is often considered an insult—to creative accountants and to their creative employers—but is it really? Is it possible for an accountant to be as creative as an artist: commercial (e.g. Andy Warhol), portrait (e.g. Andy Warhol), modern (e.g. Andy Warhol), or graffiti (e.g. anonymous)? My grandmother once taught accounting in a tertiary institution at a time when women less commonly did such things than they do now. She offered some creative as well as sensible advice to some people who wanted their accountants to be creative in their understanding of the term, rather than in the accountant's understanding of it: "The more tax you pay, the more profits you're making!" Helping to make paying tax seem like fun is perhaps even more of a creative challenge than making people want to buy a product that gives them "stronger hair"!

Zero Mostel once wonderfully creatively acted the part of a wonderfully creative play producer in Mel Brooks' movie and later stage musical *The Producers*. Zero's character inspired Gene Wilder's character—an accountant—to engage in some magnificently creative accounting that started with his own interesting theoretical observation that you can make more money out of a flop than you can out of a hit if you simply sell more than 100 percent of the show to enough investors. The show has to be a flop, because no matter how much money an oversold hit makes, it can never repay more than 100 percent of its investment. Zero's character recognized that the "scheme" at the heart of the frozen-hearted Gene's interesting theoretical observation eventually landed them both in jail, but their mutual creative expression led to them flourishing on the inside and on the outside.

Advertising requires creativity as much as authoring does, because doing it successfully means seeing new connections, such as between buying a product and getting a previously unsuspected benefit (such as "stronger hair"). Coming up with an advertising campaign to help sell something unfashionable, such as lard or philosophy, can be a wonderful creative challenge. How about:

Diet lard: 1% fat free!

or

Philosophy means the love of wisdom. So, philosophers make better lovers!

Techniques for mindfully expanding our working creativity

The creative process has led to many odd encounters, with odd progeny, and a good example is the coming together of acting training techniques and professional development techniques. This union has resulted in the development of creativity enhancing programs that can help workers to think and act more freely than they think they can.

An important benefit of workplace creativity enhancement techniques is that they can help workers to reinforce or recreate their creativity, and its rewards, by helping them to transcend their conditioned blocks. We can acquire long-term mental blocks during our process of "maturing," as we often and not necessarily accurately refer to our process of acquiring an external sense of reality. This uncreative process develops a limiting no principle, which is the opposite to our creative yes principle. Creativity enhancement techniques are actually as natural as the games that entertain and expand us as children, and they can naturally help us to get out of our deep thinking ruts, such as the belief that adults have to be serious, especially working adults, and even more es-pecially successful working adults. Creativity is fun, as well as profitable.

Techniques for enhancing workplace creativity affect the way that our brain's spread of activation mechanism works. When we think in a cautious and sequential way and are worried about real or imagined criticism, our spread of activation becomes narrow, like a tributary. When we think more freely and are motivated by enthusiasm for our opportunities, rather than by fear of consequences, our spread of acti-vation becomes wide, like a river. When we are mindful and accepting enough to let our thinking flow—naturally, deeply, and broadly—we can remove our mental blocks by allowing our thoughts to flow easily and swiftly through and around them, and to use the entire capacity of our entire being and not just the bit of it that thinks.

Flowing like a river will take us further and more rapidly in our life and working life than will trickling like a tributary, and will leave more space for others to share our journey. Workplace creativity enhancement techniques help us to create working solutions by enhancing our ability to be intuitive and to be aware of our intuitions. When we are mind-fully creative, we tend to just know things rather than having to deduce them through a painstaking analytical process. When we are mindfully creative, we can know rather than think we know, and know without thinking. Malcolm Gladwell wrote a book called *Blink: The Power of Thinking Without Thinking* that describes the power of guesses.[11] We can naturally and accurately estimate our likely success at tasks and the best way of proceeding with them, and as we get more creative, our ability to accurately guess increases because we better know ourselves, our capaci-ties, and our opportunities.

Our guessing power relates to the power of our intuition, and when this works properly, we just know that the person we are considering marrying or employing is right for us. This process takes about as long as it takes to blink, which we can also naturally do well without thinking about it. We might spend the next few days or decades agonizing over what we have done or not done, but we don't need to. Malcolm Gladwell described a situation in *Blink* when senior staff at the Smithsonian

Institution museum in Washington, D.C., were worried about the authenticity of a piece they had expensively acquired. They ran painstaking and expensive tests on it but these were not conclusive. Eventually they flew in an expert from Italy who cruised into the room the piece was stored in, correctly told them it was a fake without bothering to go any closer, then cruised back to his waiting limousine and flew back to Italy. He just knew.

Workplace creativity enhancement techniques often involve working/playing/learning to be more creative in groups because we are more creative when we are collectively creative. We often think that when people think together the result is the opposite of creativity, and we disparagingly describe this as a "herd mentality" or "groupthink." However, being in a group increases our thinking power positively as well as negatively, and journalist James Surowiecki wrote a book called *The Wisdom of Crowds* that explored this point.[12] This book describes "Why the Many are Smarter Than the Few and How Collective Wisdom Shapes Business, Economies, Societies and Nations." When enough people are asked a question, they usually collectively come up with the right answer, whether they are asked to guess the weight of a cow or the location of a sunken submarine. Surowiecki described studies done on cow weight guessing and sunken submarine location guessing where the central point of the collective guesses was more accurate than the estimates of the experts, butchers, and submarine navigators.

One particularly successful example of a workplace creativity enhancing technique, or actually a creativity freeing technique, are the "impro" corporate creativity training methods that originated in the Loose Moose Theatre Company in Vancouver. The guiding idea of "impro" style creativity enhancement is that theatrical improvisation is a great way of getting people to be collectively creative in groups by giving them some key ingredients from successful acting, workplace, and mindfulness practice:

- Be aware that your fellow actor or accountant or whoever has just included you in the growing improvisation scenario by giving you some kind of a cue.

- Accept and act upon the acting opportunity you have been given—regardless of what you might think of it. To successfully spread the improvisation creative sequence, we can't close the loop (tighten the moose noose) by not seeing, or by seeing and ignoring, our collective creative opportunities.

Brainstorming is another collective creativity enhancing technique and this has probably been around for as long as there have been brains—and for as long as there have been storms. This technique offers us much more collective creative opportunities than formal meetings do, because when we are sitting around a campfire or a boardroom brainstorming about the upcoming mastodon hunt or spring fashion range, our natural creativity isn't blocked by power structures or by other inhibiting dynamics such as seating arrangements. King Arthur was a particularly creative CEO (of ancient England) who recognized the creative power of brainstorming by installing a round table in his boardroom so his senior knights weren't inhibited by traditional seating and thinking arrangements. Brainstorming can be done informally by a group of workers in any workplace chatting together and hitting on a better way of doing something—anything—or it can be done formally in a boardroom with a sign on the opulent door magnificently stating, "Brainstorming in process. Do not enter—or risk getting swept away!"

I frequently engage in brainstorming exercises in my current workplace role as a research and evaluation person supporting a combined national, state, and local government initiative for improving preventive health. Brainstorming in my workplace is typically carried out by simply giving everyone in a room some Post-it notes and a pen, and asking them to just write down what they think is important, such as the most important potential outcome, and the best way of getting there. The Post-it notes are then stuck on a board, patterns often emerge and so do action strategies. This collective creative effort is quick and simple and can tap into the creative solutions that people are often a part of without realizing it, especially if they are worried about what others might think of their ideas as expressed in more formal ways. Brainstorming can be usefully attempted in any workplace, and in the case of my particular workplace, we have come up with strategies for improving health based on what people, including us, really think, rather than what we think they think.

You could even try a creativity enhancing workplace brainstorming/spreading technique in your workplace that brings together brainstorming principles and the active ingredient of a TV show called *Thank God You're Here!* This show was based on theater sports, and was wonderfully and instructionally creative. It didn't just encourage thinking paradigm shifts; it forced them! Actors in the show opened a door and entered a world where everybody knew what was going on, except them. They would suddenly be in an operating theater, for example, and handed a scalpel and surgical smock, and be greeted with the words "Thank God you're here!" The actors had to creatively work out what was going on and how to fit in or look like complete idiots, or both! Actually, being prepared to look like a complete idiot can be a great opportunity to break out of our usual way of doing things.

Take-to-work tips for mindful creativity

- We don't have to worry about what we think won't work out if we can just creatively wing it.
- Creativity connects people and opportunities.
- We can be naturally creative by being naturally mindful.
- We can increase our working productivity, fulfillment, and enjoyment by letting our thinking flow creatively like a running river, rather than like a trickling tributary.

Chapter 7

Mindful Enjoyment at Work

The joy of life consists in the exercise of one's energies, continual growth,
constant change, the enjoyment of every new experience.
—Aleister Crowley

It isn't possible to enjoy ourselves tomorrow or yesterday; it's only possible to enjoy ourselves now. One of the most wonderful things about being mindful, about being truly alive, is that it places us in the present moment and therefore makes life enjoyable. Does being mindful mean that we can enjoy ourselves anytime, anywhere, in any situation? Does being mindful mean that we can even enjoy ourselves at work? Work is like any other vital activity in our lives: it can be a great adventure or an ordeal, depending on how we see it and depending on our state of consciousness when we do it. To remind ourselves that it's natural to enjoy our work, all we need to do is to forget our ideas that interfere with our working enjoyment, such as that we need to struggle to succeed.

Why do anything we don't enjoy? Why live, why love, why work— why do anything that gets in the way of our natural state? Do children say, "Well, damn it all! I'd rather stay in bed, but I suppose I'd better get up and play because that's what's expected of me..."? We might think that reality is a lot grimmer than something that gives us a wonderful opportunity to do what we love, and to love what we do, but how grim our working life is depends more on our state of consciousness than on our external circumstances. Ultimately, the state of our external circumstances depends on the state of our consciousness, so it's vital we do the very best we can to make it a working asset, rather than a liability, in whatever job we are doing.

Enjoyment is something that we tend to put off until something other than what's happening right now happens, such as when we finish our current obnoxious task or get a promotion or a better job...or retire. All of these procrastinations are wasted opportunities because all we can ever enjoy is what's happening right now. You might find it naive to think that our working lives are magnificent opportunities to enjoy ourselves, and you're right—it is naive to think this—but it isn't naive to experience it.

A working enjoyment experiment

Try conducting a simple working life experiment now! Think of a working activity that you typically don't like doing—that you don't associate with enjoyment—that you would only do willingly if you were paid to do it in the form of money or prestige or promises of good things you will get in the future. This working activity might be washing the dishes, washing the dog, mowing the lawn, filling out the tax return, typing up a report, giving a public talk about something you think you don't like or understand (or that your audience won't like or understand), or it might be anything at all. Now try it while practicing some working mindfulness.

1. Start by letting go of your ideas about the job, such as that you don't like it or that it's not worth doing or that you would only do it for a considerable reward.

2. Now start doing the job, whatever it is, without any expectations about what it's going to be like doing it or what results you expect.

3. Once you've started the "job," consciously avoid giving it any mental labels, such as it being a job—with certain qualities or flavors such as "good" or "bad"—or something someone else should do or excruciatingly miserable or boring or terrific or anything other than what it really is: the experience of doing it.

4. Give the job your complete attention. Whether you're washing a dish or washing a dog or mowing a lawn or filling out a tax return or giving a public talk or whatever, don't interfere with the reality of what's actually happening here and now.

5. Consciously avoid comparing your current experiences with anything that happened in the past or that might happen in the future.

6. Consciously avoid giving your current task only some of your attention, while you give most of the rest of it (and most of the rest of your energy) to ideas about the task.

7. Really feel the working surface—the touch of the dish or dog or lawn mower handle or computer keys (or pen or quill) on your hand, or the sight of the people you're talking to—just fully experience what's happening right now.

8. Stop working when you're mindfully aware that the job feels like it's fully completed. Reflect on the experience.

Was working mindfully, no matter what at, enjoyable? Was working at something you thought you didn't like enjoyable when you did it with your full attention, energy, and opportunity for enjoyment directed at it? If your mind tries to sabotage your attempts to consistently work mindfully, enjoyably, and productively—by telling you that you don't have time, or that it's silly or useless, or whatever—just keep taking mindful working holidays (experiments, test drives) and see what happens.

The gratitude attitude

Unless you somehow acquired this book while kidnapped and doing unpaid work for a pirate gang on the South China Sea (and if you did acquire it that way, good luck!), you probably aren't officially working as a slave. You would be officially working as a slave if you were working hard at something you don't particularly like doing and not being paid for doing it and you can't escape it. Unofficial slavery is quite similar to official slavery except that you probably don't put "slave" on your tax return (and if you do, good luck!).

In previous historical times, official slavery was a common occupation and slaves were often people captured in wars or simply born into a permanent out-group, such as the non-citizens of otherwise very advanced cultures such as ancient Greece. Rural serfs weren't historically officially listed as slaves but this was a fairly academic point for a large group of illiterate and uneducated people who pretty much did everything their lordly CEOs wanted them to do even if they didn't want to. Prior to the Industrial Revolution, many people were officially and unofficially enslaved, doing particularly menial, onerous, and exhausting jobs that nowadays machines such as trucks and computers mainly do.

It might seem from our rapid information superhighway progress perspective that professional slavery is making a comeback and is a growth industry that's growing even faster than IT consultancy, but this is just a perception! A great place to start our working mindful awareness and acceptance path to working peace and enjoyment is with a gratitude attitude, so no matter what our current attitude to our current job is, at least we can be grateful that we don't work as a galley slave! There's a television show called *The Worst Jobs in History*, starring and researched by Tony Robinson, which presents re-enactments of a series of grateful-that-we-are-not-doing-them inspiring jobs such as chimney sweep, executioner, leech collector, plague burier, rat catcher, and sin eater. If you should happen to be working in any or all of these occupations, good luck!

Professional slavery comes from the opposite to the gratitude attitude, which comes from an idea that we are only working on what we are working on because we are paid to, and we would much rather be doing something else. By this definition, many of us are professional slaves, but a great tragedy or opportunity of modern life is that we don't have to be. Ultimately, our professional slavery is just an idea about reality, rather than reality, and we have the power to free ourselves from anything—even our ideas. Being professionally mindful frees us to see our job as something we would do for free, as well as for freedom, because it lets us go all the way with our natural working flow. This doesn't mean that we have to stay in the job that we are doing because it's possible to enjoy any job—we can certainly create enjoyable working and life opportunities by changing our job—but it can be useful to fully explore the enjoyment opportunities in this one first. Being professionally mindful allows us to rise above our freedom-numbing identification with our jobs, such as "I'm a production line worker" or "I'm an IT consultant" or "I'm the CEO of a public company" or "I'm a taxi driver" or, worse still, identification with the idea that we are good or bad examples of any of these things.

Michael Palin and his colleagues did a great skit on the enjoyment-lessening dangers of identifying too rigidly with our working roles in a *Monty Python's Flying Circus* episode. Palin played an army sergeant who seriously identified with his role, so much so that he thought others were as engrossed in his professional delusion as he was. After ordering his men to march around the square again and again and again, he made the hilarious and instructive mistake of offering them the opportunity to do something other than march around the square if they wanted to. Before very long, he was marching around the square by himself! When we get delusional with attachment to our ideas, including our ideas about our jobs, we end up working alone and missing out on our most important working opportunity: enjoying our working connection with our cosmic comrades.

Workplace tyrannies

Before we drive off into what can look like a dark, unknown, scary, and distant place of mindful working peace and enjoyment, it can be useful to identify some potential potholes on the road there as well as some signposts. If we are not fully enjoying ourselves at work, then we can usefully reflect on the questions "Why not?" and "What's getting in the way?" What's paralyzing us and our ability to proceed and succeed in our jobs enjoyably? What mines are lurking in our mind-field? The following list of possibilities includes some common working mindlessness traps that we can avoid if we are conscious.

Boredom

You might recognize the feeling that you've done what you're doing at work a million times before and, worse still, you don't want to do it again. This might be because you have done what you're doing a million times before or it might just feel like it.

Maybe you're bored with your job that involves opening a big box marked "Ps" and then assembling whatever's inside it into something that you put in an even bigger box marked "Qs." Maybe you're bored with your job that involves writing code for a computer that will help it do something you don't understand, care about, or like, and it feels like it's taking you longer to do it than it took whatever individual or committee (Shakespeare, Inc.?) to write the collected works of Shakespeare, or whatever individual or committee (Creation, Inc.?) to write the collected human DNA sequence. Maybe you're bored with your job that involves attending a constant stream of meetings with so many people that you can't remember their names or even care that you can't. Maybe you're simply bored with things always going badly in your job…or with things always going well.

Boredom at work is caused by our not seeing the novelty in what we are doing. Seeing the novelty in even our most repetitive jobs is what allows us consistently to do them well and enjoy them. The mindful antidote to the working tyranny of boredom is to work with complete attention—with so much attention that we won't have a chance to think we are bored, and therefore we won't be bored.

Fear

This can be seen as the opposite of boredom because it can come from caring too much about what might happen rather than not enough. We can be fearful because we are worried about what will happen if we mess up or if our crops fail or if our computer program doesn't work or if we drop the sushi or if we get the numbers wrong or if we can't find the shredder or if we fall off the stage or if we get body slammed or if we put the wrong person in jail or amputate the wrong leg. Fear is a sentence, not a word, and it's all the same sentence: hard labor.

Fear at work and fear of work are often caused by our attachment to the results of our work and often involves putting all of our awareness eggs into one imaginary consequences basket. At the level of our mind-perceived self—our ego self—we always want rewards, so we fear that the results of our actions won't be what we want them to be, and therefore won't be as rewarding as we want them to be. The mindful antidote to the working tyranny of fear is to work independently of rewards, to just do our best and enjoy the working surface and the working journey. We can accept whatever happens next by fully immersing ourselves in whatever's happening now.

Misery

Fear basically comes from our mentally "living" in the future. Misery basically comes from our mentally "living" in the past. Maybe our misery is inspired by something that we should have done at work or were going to do...but didn't. Maybe I should have accepted the job that offered more money though the people at the interview gave me bad vibes, or maybe I should have accepted the job that paid less money though the people at the interview gave me good vibes. Actually, I don't know what I should have done, only that I should have done it. If we did what we should have done or were going to do, but didn't, we would probably be enjoying ourselves a lot more, except that even if we had done it, we probably would have been miserable about that too, in our state of mindless miasma!

Misery at work is caused by non-acceptance of our working circumstances. This can manifest as soft-core resentment or as full-frontal guilt. We can enter a mental twilight zone so often that we get a season ticket to it where we just can't let go of the past, even though it's so heavy it can take all of our energy to just keep holding it up. The mindful antidote to the working tyranny of misery is to accept our past and our future by really living our present and being grateful for it. The present is a gift.

Guilt

This is a particularly extreme, damaging, and infectious form of misery but it's also a form of anger—directed inward. In a way, guilt is a form of empathy—unity—just as misery is, because if we didn't give a damn about other people, we wouldn't feel guilty about what we think we've done to them. Guilt can be seen as the dark side of empathy, and we can't construct anything real or lasting or valuable out of dark sides. Maybe we are feeling guilty at work because we did something to somebody that had terrible consequences, or that we think did. Maybe we are feeling guilty at work because we had an affair with another job, which we liked better. Whatever the reason, the mindful antidote to the working tyranny of guilt is to shine the light of our consciousness on whatever we are doing right now. How can we do more for anyone than our best at this moment?

Procrastination

I will write this section of this chapter thoroughly, magnificently, and amazingly well—later! I will dig this ditch wonderfully, just as soon as it stops raining. I will be nice to the next customer. I will do the job that I was born to do, later, when I've saved up enough money to afford it by doing the job that embarrasses me now. We all know these rationalizations for not acting until things are more conducive to action, but things will never be more conducive to action than they are right now. The mindful antidote to inaction is action, and action occurs naturally when we are aware and accepting of what is, and what we need to do with it.

Anger

We might get extremely angry in our workplace and even feel completely justified in doing so. We might get extremely angry and feel justified doing so when a work "mate" mindlessly deletes (in the blink of an iPhone) some data that we've spent hours or days typing in. We might get extremely angry when a work "mate" mindlessly removes a ladder on which we had hoped to return to dry land on. We might even get extremely angry when a work "mate" tells us the truth, or at least their truth, about our flawless new house design or business plan or sushi slice. We might get extremely angry when somebody else at work gets extremely angry, whatever the "reason." Anger comes when we feel frustrated because our idea of something that should happen isn't happening or isn't happening in the way we want it to. There are seven billion potentially different ways of doing things on this human planet, so it can be a lot easier to just go with the working flow than win seven billion arguments.

Anger is, of course, extreme non-acceptance. It comes from pain and from blaming other people for our pain. When we realize that anger comes from pain, it can help us to deal with it, in others and in ourselves. The mindful antidote to the working tyranny of anger is recognizing the working relationship between mindlessness and anger. Mindlessness results in mistakes, it results in angry reactions to mistakes, and it results in a feeling that it's okay to be actively angry with somebody even though it damages them and us.

Rigidity

Rigidity comes from being stuck in the idea that we are right and therefore that someone else is wrong. In this state, we typically go on and on playing our rigidly righteous part, no matter what the consequences: "Change?! Why should I change? I've sliced sushi/extracted teeth/busked/tiled/programed my computer this way for as long as I can remember!"

Getting stuck in the mental quicksand of the idea that we are right, and therefore everyone else is wrong, comes from being stuck in the mental quicksand of the idea that we are separate and therefore have separate optimal outcomes. This is a bit like thinking that our toes are separate and therefore have separate optimal outcomes. Working rigidity might manifest as a situation where someone with whom we are working manages to come up with a software solution for a complex computing problem, which we refuse to implement because it only works in its own way and not in the way that we have done things for years and years, and which we think must therefore be the only way. Working rigidity might manifest as our thinking that someone from whom we might learn something useful isn't worth talking to because they annoy us, but of course we don't tell anyone—including ourselves—that this is why we don't want to talk to them.

There's a story about extreme and extremely unhelpful workplace rigidity. A ship's captain recognized that he was on a collision course with another vessel one dark and stormy night and messaged, "Change your course!" at it. The other vessel didn't respond. The captain then further messaged, "According to the laws of the sea it is our right of way, so change your course immediately!" The now rapidly oncoming other vessel still didn't change its course. The captain then messaged, "We are a battleship—get out of our way!" The upcoming vessel responded, "We are a lighthouse!" The mindful antidote to rigidity is fluidity. When we open our minds and hearts by fully connecting with others, we connect with the possibility that another way of doing something, even something to which we are extremely attached, might be a better and a more enjoyable way.

When we work mindfully, we can free ourselves from all of these working tyrannies and more. To do this, we don't need to worry about sharpening particular mindfulness tools for particular working situations and responses. When we work mindfully, everything works out better for us and others automatically, including our ability to cope and even to learn and benefit when things go wrong at work, or seem to.

Mindfulness and enjoyment

Things aren't as bad as they seem—no matter how bad they seem! Even when our minds are telling us that we can't work another day or hour with the idiots we're working with or for, or doing our idiotic work. In this state, it can seem like it's easy to work mindfully, enjoyably, and productively on any job but this one and with anyone else but those we're working with! In this state, we can see our own circumstances as being the unique exception to mindfulness's enormous value...for other people! In this trans-mindfulness state, we can be totally convinced of the benefits of mindfulness, but not for us, not now, not in this particular job, and especially not at this particular stage of it.

We need to remember that our only genuine opportunity to be mindful is right now, right here, and in our current working circumstances. Ultimately, our working slavery and tyrannies come from our insidious idea of ourselves as something different from, and therefore either better or worse than, others. Any job that involves us working with or for other people, no matter how indirectly, can be enjoyable if we see it as an opportunity to be fully mindful by fully connecting with others. There are wonderful opportunities for this at work, where we can frequently share something meaningful with our colleagues—a common goal, a common challenge, a common path, a common lunchroom. Our working life will be truly enjoyable when we lighten our mind load by shedding our mind shadows, and this might well require us to work on ourselves with more diligence and inspiration than we are working on anything outside ourselves. Mindfulness and our life work will be covered in Chapter 9.

Applying mindfulness to our work, and also to our life via our work, allows us to see that our working problems, as well as our life problems, are caused by our mind-made secondary reality, rather than by our primary reality. Mindlessness enslaves us by not allowing us to see that the more we resist our job, the worse it seems, because in this state of non-acceptance we will be more likely to drift off into a dream of something else that doesn't allow us to see and appreciate what is and enjoy our real opportunities. If things are really bad in our job or we really have a bad job, then we can change it, or at least change something about it or the way we do it or, most effectively of all, we can change our attitude toward our work so that we don't just accept it but embrace it. Paradoxically, it's when we fully accept what is that we can most effectively change it. Paradoxically, it's when we stop raging and straining that we work most effectively as well as most enjoyably. This working principle was recognized way before there were courses in workplace development or in mindfulness, in sayings such as "more haste less speed," and in Jesus' enlightened work report that "My yoke is light."

When things seem to be going wrong at work perhaps because of mistakes or conflict—real and mind made—our minds wants us to speed things up and react more and more hastily...and make things even worse. Maybe we flooded the floor in the break room. Maybe we ruined a huge deal we were about to clinch because we were distracted by something more interesting happening in the break room. Maybe we charged somebody $300 too much for something they didn't particularly like anyway because we rather liked the look of another customer and weren't paying attention to our customer! You might recognize a typical mind-made response to the idea that something has gone wrong: "Quick! Do something, anything—quickly!"

This is like speeding up when we are running out of gas. It makes perfect sense to our mind but not to what knows much more than our mind—our deeper and truer selves. The mind's constant desire to be hasty rather than genuinely speedy is an important reason why workplace stress is too common and why workplace enjoyment is too rare. If we are zooming in so fast at our working target that we can't enjoy or even be aware of the ride there, in our mindless blur, then why bother going anywhere? The faster we go, the faster everything else seems to be going, and this spiral will take us where we don't want to be unless we are mindful enough to break the circuit of just reacting to stuff faster and faster. If only our minds as well as what's deeper than our minds could see that a second's reflection can save a day's or a year's stress, misery, and guilt. If only our minds could be mindful. Don't worry about worry or anything else. When we are aware at a deeper level than our minds, we are mindful all the way to and from our core.

So why do we keep rushing so fast at work, whatever our work is, that we are hardly ever actually in the same space as our job or the person with or for whom we are doing it? Maybe we are so obsessed with our deadlines that we can't see our lifelines. Maybe we mindlessly rush toward our working dead ends because we are driven by our mindless priorities that are based on our mind's unreal as well as unrealistic ideas about time and timelines.

If we can be conscious enough of our unconsciousness to realize that our work plan really consists of trading today for tomorrow, then we might realize that we are doing the same bad deal that Dr. Faustus did with his working detail devil. In Goethe's story about a man operating entirely at the level of his ego, Dr. Faustus didn't read the fine print of his diabolical deal when he sold his soul—his true self—for mind-made material riches. Any deal that involves swapping what we really have, including our enjoyable working opportunities, for what we will never have—something else—is a truly bad deal. Ultimately, no matter who has done us wrong or how often they have done it or how hard, at work or anywhere else, the mindlessness buck—of blind reaction rather than mindful response—stops with us. Knowing this makes us free.

Mindfulness, enjoyment, and working effectively

Should we really aim to enjoy ourselves at work? Surely we can only do something as serious as working effectively, grudgingly, and dourly and like "an adult," and not playfully, creatively, and enjoyably like "a child." What do you think? Better yet, what do you know? The more mindfully we do any job, the more enjoyable it will be. And the more enjoyable our job is, the better and more efficiently and productively we will do it.

There is scientific research-based evidence that enjoyment helps us to work better, as well as scientific evidence that mindfulness makes everything we do more enjoyable. A group of researchers in Canada, for example, examined the relevant research literature and found that enjoyment greatly increases our ability to sustain our activities, improve our social interactions, meet competence-demanding challenges, reduce our stress levels, and improve our psychological health.[1] In other words, enjoying our work leads to us working better and for longer, as well as more enjoyably. If we enjoy ourselves doing it, we are more likely to start a job, we are more likely to complete it, and we are more likely to fully attend to the bit between starting and completing a job, and therefore we are more likely to work well.

The research study mentioned above also demonstrated that there is a close relationship between our attitude and our enjoyment level, and between our motivation and our enjoyment level, and between our state of mindfulness and our enjoyment level. We can apply these links to our working experience because if our working attitude is based on our idea that the world owes us a living, for example, are we more or less likely to enjoy our work than if our attitude is gratitude for our working opportunity? If our working motivation comes from the belief that if we don't work we will starve, or possibly worse still, have to stay home with our spouse, are we more or less likely to enjoy our work than if we are motivated by love and enthusiasm? If our working state of mind is mindful, are we more or less likely to enjoy our work than if our working state of mind is mindless?

Being mindful makes everything that we do more enjoyable and therefore makes our entire life more enjoyable. There was a large study done at Harvard University that consisted of researchers phoning a lot of people, often, and asking them (a) How happy are you at this moment? and (b) What are you doing at this moment?[2] The results showed that people enjoy themselves more when they are fully attending to what they are doing, are fully mindful (even if they are doing something that they don't usually regard as enjoyable), than when they aren't fully attending to what they are doing (even if it's something that they usually regard as enjoyable).

Humor at work

Humor can be the most wonderful way of breaking out of our working paradigm, whether that paradigm is what we are working at or the way that we are thinking about it. How we think about our work is ultimately what leads to our working well or not quite so well, and is what makes our work enjoyable or not quite so enjoyable. "My joke is light!"

A perhaps unexpected way of working mindfully and enjoyably is to recognize that we are free to change how we look at things, including our work. This is also the active ingredient of humor: seeing things in a new, enjoyable, and funny way. Humor is a wonderful expression of mindfulness because it comes naturally when we connect with life so well, and from such a higher-than-usual perspective, that we can see that what's happening right here, right now, isn't really threatening, miserable, or annoying. When we are free to think creatively, playfully, and mindfully—by recognizing that we always have the option to be creative, playful, and mindful—what's happening right here, right now is actually brand new, spontaneous, interesting, and possibly even humorous!

We can only see the funny side of life when we really see life, and we can only do that when we are fully mindful. Seeing the humor in situations, even seemingly rotten ones, might even be the ultimate transcendence. Seeing funny sides through dark sides can be like breaking through the sound barrier to experience a new reality and new opportunities. Seeing funny sides through dark sides can even be like breaking the sound barrier, to experience the silence, stillness, and peace that lies beyond our mental noise.

There are some wonderful examples of humor as a paradigm shift. It's what black humor, in particular, is all about: enlivening and enlightening a situation that we've en-darkened by seeing it in a new and funny way. We often think, in our temporal egocentricity, that our modern generations discovered humor, as well as sex, antibiotics, and alpacas, but we didn't, and we certainly didn't invent black humor. A joke went around in a World War II Jewish ghetto:

> Jacob went for a walk one day and ran into none other than Adolf Hitler, who drew a pistol and said, "You see that pile of manure over there—eat it!" Jacob did as he was ordered, and Adolf laughed so hard that he dropped his pistol. Jacob picked up the pistol, aimed it at Adolf, and said, "Now you eat!" Jacob ran home and said to his wife, "Hey! Guess who I had lunch with today?"

Just like the other senses—sight, hearing, taste, smell, touch, "common," and "horse"—our sense of humor can be a portal that links us to a deeper and more valuable reality. Seeing the funny side of our life or working-life situation can be a great chance, and often our only chance, to get out of our life or working-life rut, and to allow for the possibility of a working solution, a paradigm shift that we may otherwise never realize.

When I was about 10 years old, my sixth grade teacher told my class one day that the most important thing to have in life is a sense of humor. I thought that was outrageous. Even at 10, I had been indoctrinated into thinking that the most important thing in life had to be serious, such as serious wealth or serious hard work or serious smartness. I went home and asked my mother what she thought of my teacher's outrageous re-mark, and she told me that he was right. A thought star was born.

Many years later, I read about a famous Irish playwright and wit who ended up in English chains on a platform at Victoria Station, about to be railroaded off to two years' hard labor for the "crime" of being homosex-ual and challenging the system that saw it as a crime. "If this is how Her Majesty treats her prisoners, she doesn't deserve to have any!" quipped Oscar Wilde. If he had seen only his chains and not an opportunity for some paradigm-shifting black humor, his chains would have chained far more than just his body.

How then can humor help us to enjoy our work, and how can being mindful help us to improve our working humor? Humor is all about seeing things in a new and potentially wonderful way. There are theories about how humor works and these are often backed up by serious sci-entific evidence, but let's ignore them and just look at a few jokes about work. Actually two of these jokes are about the same type of work, but it's potentially a particularly serious one, so it's particularly suited to being made light of. The third joke isn't really a joke but a light-heart-ed philosophical statement about the absurdity of working limitations, manifested as a running gag.

> A man goes in to see his doctor and he's not looking at all well— even less well than the other patients. He's haggard and spotty and limping and angry and looks like he might not be able to pay his bill, or want to. The doctor examines him (from a safe dis-tance) and says (loudly): "Whatever it is that you're doing, stop it!"

A woman goes in to see her doctor, and she's looking even worse than the man in the first story did. This woman, however, is possibly even luckier than the man who saw a doctor who could transcend the limitations of his professional paradigm by seeing the humor in it. This woman saw a doctor with a sense of karma. After carefully examining her, the karmic doctor cried out, "Good news! In just a few weeks you'll be a happy fish!"

In construction-related industries, there are times when you need to attach something heavy to a high point to hold it up, and you can't do it because you don't have ready access to a giant crane or magic powers. The skyhook is a mythic apparatus that you can hang stuff on, such as your hard hat, or your bracing for a heavy wall frame. It's imaginary but highly useful. There was actually a highly successful, creative, and hardworking rock band in the 1970s in Australia called Skyhooks, who were perhaps inspired in their name selection by its creatively humorous and philosophical richness.

A movie was made about a real-life doctor who used humor to inspire his patients to recover, or at least to suffer less—physically, emotionally, and spiritually—by helping them break out of the rut of their mind's reactions to their illness. The mind component of our illnesses often causes more damage than the physical components, including interference with the possibility that our illness will help us to develop at a deep life level. Our minds can convince our deeper aspects that we are experiencing a tyranny beyond our control, when it's actually this belief that's the real tyranny.

Patch Adams, as played by Robin Williams, reminds us that humor is a wonderful way of breaking through the boundaries of our habits, whether we are a patient or a doctor or the practitioner of any job that offers us a profound opportunity to deeply and rewardingly enjoy ourselves doing it, that is, all jobs. Movies may or may not have been made about dentists, accountants, sushi slicers, and salespeople helping other people to transcend their life limitations through humor—yet—but there could be! Humor helps us to transcend the limitations of what we think we can do, or should do, and being mindful helps us to see and enjoyably benefit from humor in a huge range of situations, including working ones.

Laughter can be the best working solution as well as the best medicine, and there have actually been scientific studies on how well laughter works as medicine, or at least studies of whether a sense of humor is associated with good health. A wonderful example was published in the British Journal of Health Psychology.[3] Researchers at Bond University on Australia's Gold Coast investigated the relationship between a measure of general health and a measure of a sense of humor in 504 students, general community members, and people with a medical condition. The results of this study demonstrated that there is indeed a positive association between a sense of humor and good health.

Some personal examples of mindful enjoyment at work

There are some working situations that might not look, at first fright, like opportunities for enjoyment, no matter how hard we look at them, but this appraisal largely depends on our mind's reaction to our situation rather than on the situation itself. I once lectured psychological statistics to groups of nursing students at Darwin's then newly evolved Northern Territory University, in Australia's deep north. In my first regular gig as a lecturer my classes would sometimes get just a tad challenging, dour, and even downright daunting as I tried to explain to a total group of about 100 students, most of whom were very young, that a working knowledge of the random sampling distribution of means could in some way benefit them in their eventual practice of the nursing profession.

It soon became clear to me in my early days and nights as an expat lecturer in psychology that I needed to proceed on the basis of fully attending to, and accepting, my students' actual position on such topics as the null hypothesis (H0), and the alternative hypothesis (H1), rather than proceeding on the basis of what I thought their position should be.

Once I stopped thinking and started responding, it was soon clear that my rigid logic wasn't meeting the real need that I needed to meet and this was making us all miserable! I realized that I had to be a lot more creative in my approach to teaching and communication than what I was being, and this was the beginning of my reasonably successful season in the tropical sun as a stand-up stats performer. My statistical jokes and excursions, such as the applied probability evening at the then Mindil Beach Casino, often didn't have quite their intended effect, but the students were soon mindful that I was at least trying to be something other than mindlessly inappropriate in my approach to them. Working together with my students was much more enjoyable, and educational, than working apart had been.

There is, of course, a professional danger, or rather a potential working adventure, that might confront us when we attempt to contribute toward an increase in working enjoyment in creative ways such as by the strategic and also natural use of humor or camaraderie. We might fail! We might fail miserably and embarrassingly—at least on the surface. When I gave my first Experimental Psychology Conference presentation as a PhD student, I decided that I would start things off with an experimental psychological joke (and these are not especially easy to devise). The fruit of this effort was met with myriad dour and accusing stares that I never quite recovered from—at one level. But at another level, I learned that all we need to do is what we think is right, even if that's trying to be light when everyone else is trying to be heavy. Recognizing that we can't control outcomes, and that our life and work will be much more enjoyable if we can trust in our life's deeper meaning, or humor, can help us to enjoy life on the wings of this moment. Working wisdom means knowing that we are just playing a part, that we are already a working whole. Ultimately, all we need to do is our best and enjoy doing it, no matter what we are doing.

Some techniques for improving our workplace enjoyment

Mindful working enjoyment is just the same as any other sort of enjoyment: we are more likely to enjoy ourselves, and more likely to enjoy ourselves at work, if we are mindful. Anything we do to increase our mindfulness and the mindfulness of those with whom we work will help to create a more enjoyable workplace. We don't need to put mindfulness in our office's drinking fountain or whisky bottle, although it might help things along enormously if we did. Mindfulness is naturally infectious in a good way, just as smiles are and humor is, so the best and easiest way to improve our workplace's enjoyment is to improve our enjoyment.

Treat your next working day as an experiment in working enjoyably. Don't worry about whether it works out or not; it's just an experiment.

- Try smiling at people—even if they haven't smiled at you first—even if you think you don't like them or they don't like you. If you've only packed three smiles, then give them to the three people you think you like least!

- Think less about your job and realize more...that work is a wonderful opportunity to enjoy life, with others and for others.

- Give people stuff that you would like to be given—advice, attention, affection, directions, anything—and see what happens.

- Don't criticize, no matter what happens and no matter what you think happens.

- Try sharing a joke rather than a complaint with a fellow worker. Carp and you carp alone; laugh and the whole world laughs with you—or at least at you!

- Try asking yourself, "How can I better enjoy myself and help others to better enjoy themselves today?" rather than, "How can I do more stuff today?"

- Really believe in the value of your workplace and your fellow workers. Good and happy teams aren't made up of people who think they should be in a better team.

Here's a story about a group of tired monastery workers (monks) in a tired monastery on a large mountain. They couldn't do anything with any energy, except go downhill. (This story can be adapted into an instructive scenario for any workplace—even for your workplace.) The CEO of the monastery couldn't work out why their profits were going downhill even faster than their spirits were. No one in the nearby village listened to them or respected them anymore, or even bought their wine. The monks were miserable and getting old fast. They weren't taking on any spiritual apprentices because the young people in the nearby village all wanted to do stuff that looked more exciting than praying and meditating and chanting and making wine all day. In desperation, the CEO of the mountain monastery visited a rival monastic outfit that seemed to be withstanding the spiritual downturn better than his outfit was, and he asked for some advice.

"There is among you a great spiritual worker!" said the rival CEO.

The CEO galloped back home to his monastery on his now enthusiastic donkey and told his fellow monks the good news. All of a sudden, they were energized and intrigued, and were all constantly wondering which of them was the great spiritual worker. In hardly any time at all, the monastery was full of happy and profitable monks who realized that each of them was a great worker!

Take-to-work tips for mindful enjoyment

- We really don't need to be so obsessed with our working deadlines that we can't see our working lifelines.

- Enjoyment works, even at work.

- Have fun doing what you're doing, and try the working equivalent of adlibbing—working without an idea script or a safety net—and just find out what happens.

- Enjoyment is our natural state and our natural working state when we are mindful. This just means being fully alive to the present moment, waking up to ourselves, and waking up to our enjoyment of what is, now, at work.

Chapter 8

Some Working Examples of Mindfulness

The things of this world draw us where we need to go.
—Mary Rose O'Reilley

The working principles of mindfulness presented in this book can help anybody to do any job more successfully and enjoyably than they are currently doing it. The working principles of mindfulness also apply specifically to specific jobs, and to specific groups of jobs, and this knowledge might be particularly helpful to people who work in these jobs, or who know someone who does, or who hope (or fear!) that they might eventually work in any or all of them. This chapter will describe how being mindful can help you to perform well and happily in some particular jobs as examples of how you can perform well and happily in any job. Some working life lessons from some particular jobs will be presented, from people working in them who are at least occasionally mindful enough to recognize the difference between mindfulness and mindlessness, and to realize which works better.

Hospitality

Knowledge is knowing a tomato is a fruit.
Wisdom is not putting it in a fruit salad.
—Miles Kington

People who work in the hospitality industry include wait staff, bar staff, motel/hotel workers, cooks and chefs, and many more, including those who work in hospitality and don't get paid for it, and also those who do get paid for it but who don't feel hospitable! The hospitality industry is huge and is fuelled by people's need to eat and drink and sleep and otherwise be looked after in public places. Unlike many other industries, which depend on ongoing demand for and supply of natural resources such as uranium and oil, the hospitality industry is more universal and depends on unlimited natural resources such as human heartfulness and mindfulness. These unlimited natural resources help people to serve themselves through serving others—even those they think don't deserve it! Hospitality is a broad church indeed and most professional positions include at least occasional elements of hospitality, or should. All kinds of hospitality workers can benefit from applying mindfulness principles to their work.

What makes a good hospitality worker good and a good one better?

According to ancient wisdom traditions, we find out who we really are by finding out who we really aren't. It's a bit like that with hospitality. We can get a pretty good idea of what a good hospitality worker is like once we've figured out what a bad one is like. There are plenty of examples of bad hospitality workers, and they tend to stand out more than good examples do, especially when they're funny examples. There's something intrinsically hilarious about people who hate people and who hate giving while working in jobs where it's rather hard to avoid both of these things. You might have had an inhospitable hospitality experience yourself, such as when you thought that the behavior of the waiter, hotel employee, chef, or customers was so horrendously awful that they must have been a personal enemy, until you realized that you had only been in downtown Ulan Bator for about an hour and really hadn't had time to make any enemies!

The essence of successfully working in the hospitality industry is really just the essence of giving—expanding yourself through acts of generosity and service to others, rather than contracting yourself through acts of meanness and revenge often aimed at ourselves via others. Santa Claus is a great example of a tirelessly giving hospitality worker; he doesn't even get tips or care about not getting them. We don't have to be quite so magnificently ostentatious in our acts of kindness to realize through our mindful hospitality, or lack of it, that what we give to others we give to ourselves. This principle explains why it's particularly useful for hospitality workers to not have murderous self-intent!

Mindfulness and hospitality

It's even more useful for hospitality workers to pack some mindfulness into their tool kits than to pack smiles! Hospitality expert Jennifer Ritchie wrote an article about the benefits of mindfulness in entertainment and hospitality, and described such important successful attributes of hospitality workers as the magic touch, the ability to add something special to a hospitality experience that helps its givers stand out from the mindless crowd.[1] Ritchie made the important point that a wonderful thing about being in a nice restaurant, hotel, or vacation spot is that we are often more easily mindful there—we really hear the singing of the birds at twilight and the popping of the champagne cork in the later hours! These experiences contrast starkly with those of not clearly hearing our alarm clock screeching or our boss ticking.

No matter where we are visiting or staying, and no matter how wonderful it is, the real active ingredient of successfully being in a vacation mindset is the attentiveness—the mindfulness—of the people whose job it is to look after us and respond to our needs. Realizing this can help hospitality workers to work more mindfully, successfully, and enjoyably.

The key to providing good service is simply giving complete attention to who we are serving and not letting our mutual mindful reality spell get broken by non-core thoughts, such as seeing our next customer, as providing our best and last chance to get back at the universe or, worse still, at ourselves via others!

Some life lessons that we can learn best hospitably

Where better to learn the value of service than by working in the hospitality industry? Where better to learn the truth that what we do to others we do to ourselves than in a job that forces us to experience existential intimacies? The Islamic wisdom tradition gives us some great, if possibly a tad extreme, hospitality industry advice: if our enemy is our guest, and our friend comes into our house to kill our enemy, it is our duty to defend our enemy to the death from our friend—because he or she is our guest! If you're working in a particularly grim bar and regarding your customers as your guests, this advice might seem a bit challenging, but the spirit is clear even if the beer might not be. I was once the voluntary leader of a voluntary tea and coffee team serving people on a spiritual path who might have been expected to be grateful for anything they got, even lukewarm coffee.

"This isn't strong enough!"

"But I wanted a latte!"

"It's too hot!"

My advice to my fellow unpaid hospitality workers when the voluntary going got tough was "Service is the shortcut to enlightenment!"

When the voluntary going got even tougher, I tried another tack: "Tell them that if they don't like the product or the service or the price, they can go to our competition!" (We didn't have any.)

A mini interview with a mindful hospitality worker

Interviewer: What's the most important attribute of a good hospitality worker?

Mindful hospitality worker (at least occasionally!): In hospitality, the most important attribute is selflessness. This is best exercised through service. Service is paramount, and I don't just mean transporting drinks or delivering food. What I mean here is giving wholeheartedly of yourself in every aspect of the encounter you have with your guest. You need to like people and be genuinely interested in diversity. You need to enjoy teamwork, as you will spend a greater part of your time with your comrades.

Int: How might mindfulness help hospitality workers work better and more enjoyably?

MHW: In hospitality, being mindful can help you to put aside that grumbly, reluctant, judgmental self and create a connection of true interaction with your guests. The experience for all parties involved then becomes of a much higher quality, more authentic, and fun.

Int: Do you have any anecdotes that might illustrate a mindful and/ or mindless approach to working in hospitality?

MHW: There were situations where I needed to be fully attentive to the needs of guests and be genuinely willing to fulfil them, even when I'd been on my feet for 10 hours, and my back hurt, and the people at the dinner party were being impatient and demanding. Hospitality is a bit like my other job, acting: the show must go on because the show's bigger than how I'm feeling!

Sales

The secret of many a man's success in the world resides in his insight into the moods of men and his tact in dealing with them.

—J.G. Holland

People who make stuff or who teach people stuff or who fix people can argue that making stuff, teaching people stuff, and fixing people are the most important things we can do and get paid for doing, because where would we be without stuff, knowledge, and health? People who sell stuff, however, can reasonably argue that selling is the most important profession because what good is anything to anybody, whether goods or service or spiritual messages or whatever, if they don't have it—because they haven't bought it?

A heavily laden branch of the selling industry is reputed to be the world's oldest profession, and selling has certainly been around for as long as there have been people who have less than they need or want while other people have more than they need or want. Selling is like a lot of other jobs in that there are a lot more people doing it, at least sometimes, than the ones who get paid for it (at least occasionally!). No matter what job we are officially doing, some kind of selling is usually an important part of it. We all need to sell our actions, ideas, and reasons to somebody at some time. All kinds of sellers can benefit from applying mindfulness principles to their work.

What makes a good seller good and a good one better?

The essence of being a good seller is similar to the essence of being a good actor or missionary. To successfully sell anything to anybody else, we firstly need to sell it to us; we need to believe in it. I was once sold a ticket in Kathmandu airport for a sightseeing flight over and around but hopefully not through the high Himalaya that separates Nepal and Tibet. I and several other particularly gullible future passengers could have simply bought a ticket from the ticket desk, but a ticket-selling tout persuaded me to pay him more than the going rate because the seat he proposed selling me was uniquely magnificent. His face, body, and entire being radiated sincerity, love, and enthusiasm. I still haven't worked out whether this love was genuinely for me and my mountain-viewing pleasure prospects, or for my money, but the point of this sales story is that this guy was a magnificent seller because he truly believed in his product. Truth sells, not deception.

Mindfulness and selling

Good sellers can seem to be a lot of things, and not all of them are positive, but being a good seller is like being a good anything else: success comes from a place deep within us, deeper than cunning or cleverness or unscrupulousness or the ability to manipulate. Being a genuinely good seller, which means being able to sell again and again—even, and especially, to the same person—comes from really believing in what we are selling. To sell anything, we have to believe in it, and at a deeper level, we need to sell ourselves by believing in ourselves.

Martin Seligman is a famous American psychologist who published a very influential book, especially in psychological circles, way back in 1975, about learned helplessness.[2] It was particularly lucky for me in the early 1980s that Martin Seligman had taken the trouble to write this book. I was doing a PhD in psychology at the time and was rather ambitiously trying to come up with a unified theory not only of how the human mind works, but also how less well-publicized bits of us such as our emotions fit in. As if that wasn't enough, I was also using this model to attempt to describe and predict psychopathology, including depression.

One of the key theories of depression that I modeled was Seligman's theory of learned helplessness. According to this theory, we get depressed when we learn, or think we learn, that nothing we do works out well so we might as well stay home in bed. This is how an unfortunately large number of us spend our time. Fifteen years after publishing *Learned Helplessness*, Seligman published its happy ending: *Learned Optimism*.[3] This book is an important contribution toward the recent positive psychology movement, and its basic idea is that yes, we can learn helplessness—which can make us depressed—but wait, there's more! The antidote to learned helplessness is that we can also learn optimism, and we can learn (or actually remember) happiness.

Optimism is a vital component of successful selling. Even more broadly, optimism is a vital component of successful living. Optimism links mindfulness and the ability to successfully sell a whole range of stuff because when we are mindful, we are naturally optimistic: we focus on what is, rather than dwell on our thoughts about what's wrong with what is. When we are mindful, we are naturally optimistic because in this state, we automatically realize that there's nothing wrong with what is when we fully tune into it, fully give it a chance to be more than what we think it is. Optimism links selling with a vital practice for perfecting a happy life and a happy working life. We believe in our lives and in our work, and in our life and work products so well that we can sell them, firstly to ourselves. After all, if Jesus and the Buddha and Mohammed hadn't believed that they knew something so good and true about life that they could help others and themselves with it, they wouldn't have sold their messages, and people in their age and in ours would be less happy than they are.

According to Seligman, the only predictor of whether someone will be a good seller is whether or not they are optimistic, whether they have a natural resilience that comes from their belief in the basic goodness of themselves or of their lives or even of their luck. Seligman laid his conceptual cards on the reality roulette table and approached a huge U.S. insurance company, MetLife, with an invitation to trial the personnel selection tests they routinely used to select salespeople against his selection test, which was a simple test of optimism. The company eventually agreed to this offer and soon found that Seligman's test worked much better than theirs did, so they implemented it and made millions of dollars from their increased sales power. Mindfulness sells as well as tells!

Some life lessons that we can learn best as a mindful seller

Where better to learn the value of letting go of our stuff than by selling it? Things pass, whether we want them to or not, whether they are on special or not, and things can also go stale if we try to stockpile them and don't let them pass. Successful selling is all about recognizing the natural flow of things—into and out of us, from surplus to scarcity and back again.

Where better to learn the value of listening to people—recognizing our essential oneness with them—than by trying to sell something to somebody we don't like or don't want to listen to or whose needs we aren't interested in? Mindless selling might indeed be an act of mutual misery, but mindful selling can be an act of combined contentment! Where better than in selling or attempted selling to learn the value of being free of our attachments to the results of what we do? I once sold ice creams at the Sea Lake show, in a hot and dusty rural region called the Mallee, and was paid 5 cents a circuit of the oval in the hot sun for the privilege. This might sound like a fabulous amount of money for a rather young person all those years ago, but it's actually even less than what I'm being paid now, and my ice cream eating bill greatly exceeded my salary. The point of this selling story is that sometimes we can profit more by not getting what we want or not being able to sell what we would like to sell or not doing what we would like to do, than we can profit from getting what we want. Selling or attempted selling can teach us better than just about anything else can that all we can do is offer!

A mini interview with a mindful seller

Interviewer: What's the most important attribute of a good seller?

Mindful seller (at least occasionally!): The ability to listen fully to the customer.

Int: How might mindfulness help sellers to work better and more enjoyably?

MS: In a state of open awareness, we can pay full attention to the customer when they are explaining their need. Selling is a misnomer; it's really all about listening—hearing the customer fully then restating their need so they feel understood and affirmed. This is easy and enjoyable when the salesperson is fully present. Making full eye contact helps us to connect with the essential humanity of the customer and recognize that their need is actually our need.

Int: Do you have any anecdotes that might illustrate a mindful and/or mindless approach to working in sales?

MS: I worked for some years as the manager of a surf shop, and I noticed that often the staff, myself included, would literally size up the customers for the wet suits they wanted, rather than ask them the right questions about what their needs were, about how often they would surf, in what sort of conditions, for how long. The customers knew when they weren't really being listened to and they would often tell us afterward that we hadn't sold them what they really needed. The lesson here is that one size doesn't fit all! I asked my staff to just ask our customers four questions, and to remember their answers and feed them back to them—it worked!

Teaching

Those who know, do. Those that understand, teach.

—Aristotle

If selling is sometimes sold as the oldest profession and lawyers can make a case that law is the oldest profession, then teachers can legitimately ask who taught sellers to sell, and who taught lawyers to make their cases? The teaching profession includes people who teach anybody anything and get paid for it. There are also a great many teachers who teach at least something to somebody as part of their job without being called teachers, such as sports coaches, life coaches and various trainers, and there are even more people who regularly teach something to somebody and don't get paid for it. All kinds of teachers can benefit from applying mindfulness principles to their work.

What makes a good teacher good and a good one better?

The essence of teaching anybody anything actually isn't teaching, odd as that might seem. Nobody can teach anybody anything, even if we think we can. The essence of teaching is helping people to learn, and the best teachers are the ones who are self-aware enough to know this. Good teachers are, like good examples of any profession, light on their mental feet. Being light on your mental feet means being mindfully agile enough to get out of the way of your thoughts—such as about how well or badly you are doing—before they land on you! Good teachers just do what they're doing without needing to create their sense of self through it, such as by thinking, "I'm a teacher, and a damned good/bad one at that!" Good teachers transcend their selves: "I help others to realize their full potential to be more than what they think they are, by firstly being more than I think I am!"

The Canadian political economics professor and humorous writer Stephen Leacock was reputedly once more famous than his country—which says something interesting about him or his country, or both. Leacock wrote a story in the early 20th century that was based on a common and simplistic notion of teaching as forcing stuff on people, often on those who don't particularly want it inflicted on them. His 1910 scenario of future teaching revealed a profession that had "progressed" so far that students didn't have to do something as puerilely primitive as sit in classrooms all day, absorbing lessons. Maybe even in 1910 it was recognized, at least by Leacock, that teaching is done best when it facilitates rather than tries to force-feed learning, and this works best with the active cooperation of the taught. He perhaps presciently pointed out a problem with the passive learning model when he portrayed future teachers as simply giving their students a series of operations—as in literally transplanting stuff into their brains, much as mobile phone apps are literally transplanted into the modern mobile phone brain. Most of these teaching operations were quite painless, but some were quite painful, such as trigonometry!

Teaching isn't something that any of us do; it's something that we can help happen. People want to learn—whether they are seemingly recalcitrant CEOs not fully tuning into the learning possibilities offered by a hot new mindfulness program or seemingly recalcitrant apprentices not fully tuning into the learning possibilities offered by a hot new training program. Teaching can be a particularly valuable opportunity for people to learn many important things about life (including how to live mindfully), for both the teachers and for the taught.

Mindfulness and teaching

Education consultant Deborah Schoeberlein published a useful book on mindfulness and teaching in which she mentions that a great advantage of mindfulness practice for teachers is that it changes their perception of time.[4] Time, or actually our mind's perceived lack of it, is a big cause of stress, especially in a profession where there doesn't seem to be enough of the stuff to do what we want—as teachers, parents, educators, government, and children. These groups of people's only commonality might be the perception that there isn't enough time to do it, whatever it is! Schoeberlein described how schools compress time, or seem to, and she advocates a simple mindfulness technique—pausing and taking a deep breath—to help teachers to stop getting caught up in time or the apparent lack of it. Once we recognize and accept that schools (and also many other workplaces) have a timetable, then we can find freedom within this reality rather than find stress by not recognizing it and by not accepting it.

Some life lessons that we can learn best as a mindful teacher

Any job can help us to learn valuable lessons, and teaching is a particularly valuable way to spend our time—and to learn the lessons of timelessness. There is an old saying: "If you can't do something, teach it!" Certainly teaching is a wonderful opportunity to learn about all kinds of things, including ourselves and other people, and how we can best help each other to learn what we need to learn.

Teaching is a particularly good opportunity to learn about leadership. Good teachers are usually also good leaders because they don't try to drag people to learning; they inspire it. The best teaching is like the best leadership: done by example.

Teaching is also a great opportunity to learn about patience. Good teachers are patient above all else, because if we are not imposing something on others, then we have to wait for them to discover it for themselves. Waiting is something that can be done while looking at our watch and counting time, through clenched teeth, or it can be done by just allowing things, including our natural wisdom, to grow in time. There's an obscure Buddhist saying: "Every blade of grass will be enlightened." This doesn't mean that we can't help grass to grow by dropping some fertilizer on it, or help to teach gardeners how to grow grass better, but ultimately we can't force-feed water to a thirsty horse (or camel!) or garden, so patience is paramount. It can help us to be patient if we can step back from what's biting our toes and see the big picture of what we are working toward, and therefore how we can best get there and help others to get there. There are times when we can help people best by telling them, and there are times when we can help people best by showing them, and then there are times when we can help people best by just getting out of their way.

A mini interview with a mindful teacher

Interviewer: What's the most important attribute of a good teacher?

Mindful teacher (at least occasionally!): To be able to communicate well and to love what we are teaching.

Int: How might mindfulness help teachers to work better and more enjoyably?

MT: You can't be aware of what's going on with the people you're teaching unless you're aware yourself. Mindfulness can be really useful for teachers because it can help us to recognize when people we are teaching start to lose their awareness—before they go to sleep!

Int: Do you have any anecdotes that might illustrate a mindful and/or mindless approach to working as a teacher?

MT: This is a bit embarrassing, but I once asked an 11th-grade student to play a DVD without asking him what it was first, and he played a pornographic one! I wouldn't have done that if I had been mindful. On the positive side, there have been quite a lot of times when I just didn't know the answer to a student's question, but there was one time when I didn't get flustered but just stayed calm and aware as if I knew the answer would come from somewhere. A student who usually didn't say anything in class came up with an answer—a really good answer—and it seemed like my calmness helped her to give us her answer.

The trades

Nothing in the world can take the place of persistence. Talent will not; nothing is more common than unsuccessful men with talent. Genius will not; unrewarded genius is almost a proverb. Education will not; the world is full of educated derelicts. Persistence and determination alone are omnipotent.

—Calvin Coolidge

A lot of very different people work in a lot of very different trades, but a common element of many of them is that they tend to involve the performance of practical activities such as building things or fixing them or making things work or making things work better. People who work in trades include carpenters, plumbers, electricians, builders, concreters, hairdresser, fitters and turners, and many, many others. One of my grandmothers once had a friend who made a conscious decision that none of her offspring would go to higher learning institutions but would all learn trades, no doubt to protect them from whatever wickedness she thought lurked beneath the university cloisters. Although my grandmother had no fear of higher learning institutions herself, and indeed she taught in one, my grandmother greatly respected this practical attitude. As with many of the jobs mentioned here, the distinction between being a professional and an occasional tradesperson is often fuzzy because most of us occasionally do at least some of the practical things that tradespeople do frequently.

What makes a good tradesperson good and a good one better?

The essence of being a good tradesperson is skill, and skill is partly something that we can work on and partly something that we can work with. In other words, skill is something that can be taught to us or developed in us through appropriate training, but this learning process will work better if we are working with rather than against our natural talents. Skill can be improved by improving our general working knowledge as well as by improving our knowledge specific to particular jobs, and practical working knowledge includes the ability to concentrate for long periods of time and to not waste energy working against our natural focus. Mindfulness can greatly improve our specific skill level as well as our general working knowledge by helping us to successfully work at what we mean to do, and not get distracted into doing what we don't mean to do.

The difference between a not-so-good tradesperson, a good tradesperson and a great tradesperson is partly their skill level but also their motivation. It's unlikely that we'll be really good at anything we attempt unless we have a deep affinity for it and a real desire to do it. A strong working relationship with whatever we are working on comes partly from mindfully doing it, and also from mindfully realizing that what we are working on is the best expression of our deeper self and purpose. Whether or not we are doing the work that works best for us and others can be more obvious in the trades than in many other jobs because the trades often involve our creating or shaping or fixing something tangible that other people can see too. A bad haircut or driveway is as obvious as a good haircut or driveway.

Good tradespeople usually link well with other people, as well as with their tools of trade and with their working surfaces—often so well that their bodies, minds, and spirits fully extend into their jobs and beyond them. Deep human connectedness allows good tradespeople to recognize and meet deep human needs, including their customers' and employer's needs, and to be naturally and successfully reliable, trustworthy, and solution-oriented.

Mindfulness and the trades

The trades have been getting a bit unfashionable lately, as demonstrated by the eradication of technical schools and "shop" classes in the United States. According to Matthew Crawford in his book *The Case for Working With Your Hands*, this phenomenon is caused by modern societies wanting "knowledge workers" rather than manual workers.[5] Maybe this preference is caused by our being so seduced by our thoughts about what knowledge looks like that we are forgetting what knowledge is, and this includes knowledge of how to do things. The trades can be great opportunities to practice mindfulness and great opportunities to live life with a sense of full purpose and working reality because they involve actually doing real stuff that either works or doesn't work. No amount of argument or theoretical justification will make a faulty electrical circuit right or a bad haircut good.

A great primer for helping people work in the trades mindfully, successfully, and enjoyably (especially the mechanical trades!) is *Zen and the Art of Motorcycle Maintenance*, published in 1974.[6] This book was based on the even more ancient working mindfulness classic, *Zen in the Art of Archery*, published in 1948.[7] The gist of both these books is that working is a fast track to enlightenment, especially when we are working at something real and simple, such as motorcycle maintenance and archery, and especially when we allow our natural flow of energy to manifest through some real and simple work. If we are a part-time seeker of ultimate truth and also a part-time university lecturer, then we can argue that our life theory or university theory is right because no one can prove that it isn't. If we are a part-time seeker of ultimate truth and also a part-time motorcycle mechanic or archer, then if our theory is wrong, or unnecessary, we will break down on the road to nirvana or miss our truth target!

Some life lessons that we can learn best as a mindful tradesperson

Where better than in the trades to learn the value of constantly and completely giving our attention to our working surface, to the feel of our paintbrush or scissors? A great advantage of working with stuff that's so real that other people can see it too—any other people and not just experts or other people sharing our working delusion—is that this is a valuable journey to real results, in general life as well as in working life.

A mini interview with a mindful tradesperson

Interviewer: What's the most important attribute of a good tradesperson?

Mindful tradesperson (at least occasionally!): The ability to be present to the task at hand while also being aware of his/her immediate environment.

Int: How might mindfulness help people to work better and more enjoyably as tradespeople?

MT: By helping them to work in the here and now (rather than in the not here, not now!) with focused, open awareness. This allows us to be at ease while being aware of risks and hazards in the workplace and of those people working around us. Being aware also helps us to remember to stop work occasionally and be present to assess progress in the context of the overall task, without attachment or anxiety about the result.

Int: Do you have any anecdotes that illustrate a mindful and/or mindless approach to working as a tradesperson?

MT: We once thought we had to break up some clay rocks under the hot sun, to prepare the ground for a path, and we were exhausted before we'd even started the job because we had ideas about what the job would be like, how hard it would be. It turned out that we weren't asked to do that job and instead we did some work inside in the shade. That made us realize that we can so easily get unnecessarily worried and exhausted by breaking rocks in our minds!

The creative and performing arts (and sciences)

Life's but a walking shadow, a poor player that struts and frets his hour upon the stage, and then is heard no more.

—William Shakespeare, *Macbeth*

The creative and performing arts (and sciences) include a lot of jobs, including some that people get paid for doing. Some examples of this broad and fuzzy genre include musicians, writers, publishers, artists, filmmakers, actors, dancers, and various others of us who make and populate scenes.

What makes a good creative and performing arts (and sciences) worker good and a good one better?

There's a magical secret ingredient of successful and enjoyable creative and artistic performance. It may well be a "trade secret," but there are tantalizing public clues offered about it in the working jargon of many creative and artistic professions. Musicians have been known to refer to whatever it is that lets them do what they're doing well as their "mojo" or "vibe." Writers have also risen to the challenge of describing this indescribable something as "access to their muse." But whatever the magical and secret ingredient of successful artistic and creative performance is and is called, it's a flow state. Being able to go with, rather than against, our natural flow is a vital part of working successfully and enjoyably at many jobs, not just officially creative or performing ones.

Whether our creative or performance professional activity is music or science or whatever, a principle of success is that the harder a creative person tries to be creative, or a performing person tries to perform, the worse they usually do. Successful creative performance often comes from just getting out of the way of our real creative force, sending our ego off on annual leave, and allowing the real worker—our deeper selves—to simply express what they truly are. Great musicians such as Bach and Mozart described their music making as acts of listening; they didn't compose anything, they transcribed it. In other words (or notes), they just allowed the universe to make its music through them. Great artists and sculptors have said much the same thing and so did a great scientist, Albert Einstein, who described his ability to just see solutions as an act of knowing and not of doing.

Mindfulness and the creative and performing arts

The relationship between mindfulness and creativity was described in Chapter 6, and there are also some great primers for helping people to work mindfully, successfully, and enjoyably in the creative and performing arts. These are the same primers that help people work mindfully, successfully, and enjoyably in the trades—*Zen and the Art of Motorcycle Maintenance*,[8] and *Zen in the Art of Archery*.[9] The creative and performing gist of both of these books is that we get into a creative flow when we transcend our minds and their worries and just do. *Zen and the Art of Motorcycle Maintenance* was rejected by 121 publishers before it was published—a world record for a bestseller—and it went on to sell over five million copies. This creative sales information perhaps illustrates the most important quality of greatness in any field: having the extreme good or bad taste to believe in something that others don't.

Some life lessons that we can learn best as mindful creative or performing artists

Where better than the creative and performing arts to recognize and expand on a subtle life energy that goes all the way down to our working core? This subtle working energy is a creative force that's vital to the work of many occupations, including ones that we officially designate as belonging to the creative and performing arts. What is it that allows people doing many jobs to recognize a deep flow that allows them to reach all the way to the source of their being and to ultimate job satisfaction? We can all tap into the source of our true identity as creators and created, and this process can be wonderfully expressed in wonderfully creative work performance in any fertile field.

A mini interview with a mindful actor

Interviewer: What's the most important attribute of a good actor?

Mindful actor (at least occasionally!): To be a good actor, you must be willing (and able) to step out from behind your protective layers. You need to move beyond the limits of who you present yourself as and see if something else is possible. You must listen really intently to your fellow actors and follow where the moment beckons you. During my earlier years as a drama student, one of our teachers espoused this philosophy which I think sums it up nicely: Risk—Trust—Allow.

Int: How might mindfulness help actors to work better and more enjoyably?

MA: In acting, mindfulness can free you from the anxieties of performance. You can open yourself to the possibilities of the moment instead of overlooking them by sticking rigidly to your ideas of how things should go.

Int: Do you have any anecdotes that illustrate a mindful and/or a mindless approach to working as an actor?

MA: We were rehearsing a play once, and for the life of us, a fellow actor and myself could not get a scene we were in together to make any sense. No matter what we tried, it always sounded disjointed and false. After weeks of trying to work it out, we agreed to just rush through our lines and hope that the audience wouldn't notice too much. On opening night, at the arrival of the scene, I remember walking toward my fellow actor and actually seeing him as I never had before. I remember all of my lines disappearing from my mind and being very aware of the subtle differences in the way I was moving. I waited in this elongated moment before I spoke, then I opened my mouth and the first line came out completely different to how I had always previously delivered it in rehearsal. My fellow actor responded so fluently and appropriately, and the scene flowed forth in this perfectly natural way. We stopped trying and it just came out right. This event gave us a great deal of confidence and the play went on to have a terrific run.

The legal industry

Make crime pay. Become a lawyer.
—Will Rogers

People who work in the broad law industry include law clerks, legal secretaries, lawyers, and judges. With the possible exception of the United States, where approximately half the world's lawyers can be found, wild and free in their natural habitat, only a small percentage of the world's workforce work as lawyers. For some deep psychological reason that I don't want to risk a libel suit by speculating on, there are probably more lawyers per square inch of film screen and novel page than there are members of just about any other profession. Lawyers on the film screen and novel page are sometimes heroes and sometimes villains, just as current or ex real-life lawyers are. Some famous ex-qualified lawyers include the extremely diverse threesome of former U.S. President Richard Nixon, former rock star Peter Garrett, and former peaceful revolutionary Mahatma Gandhi.

Although not all that many of us work officially as lawyers, law is important to all of us because things work out a lot better for us and for others if we are working with it, and not against it—whether the law is natural or legal.

What makes a good legal professional good and a good one better?

My wife and I went to a young professionals' development week in upstate New York during our honeymoon, even though I wasn't particularly young or professional at the time. There were several professional streams operating there including law, and the group of lawyers was a particularly interesting group of people. At dinner one night, I asked the assembled group of young lawyers what a suitable collective name would be for members of their profession and humbly suggested "a pride of lawyers." They rather liked this idea, but whatever they are known as collectively, the young professional development legal group were told by their stream leader that there is only one talent that is required of a successful lawyer, and only one attribute: intelligence. I have since broadened my inquiry into the natural laws of lawyers and ascertained that perhaps the most important attribute of a good lawyer isn't intelligence in its usual psychological meaning, but human intelligence, which includes the ability to deeply listen to other humans.

Mindfulness and the legal profession

Being able to simply be aware and accepting of what we are aware of, i.e. mindful, is increasingly being recognized as of particular usefulness for certain professions, including the legal profession. The prestigious Berkeley University in California has devised a Berkeley Initiative for Mindfulness in Law, which is an "innovative new center at Berkeley Law exploring the benefits of meditation to legal education and law practice."[10] The program offers specific legal profession applications of mindfulness—both formal and informal—such as explorations of "the parallel paradigm shifts invited by the practices of mindfulness and restorative justice, as well as the place of forgiveness in restorative processes." Such programs stem from the natural association between mindfulness practice, empathy toward other people, and the natural human justice that these attributes foster separately and together. Berkeley law students are being offered an elective course in mindfulness and law that culminates in them drafting their own plan of how they will integrate mindfulness into their study and eventual practice of law.

The U.S. Institute for Mindfulness Studies (IMS) offers "mindfulness insights and instruction in techniques specifically designed for attorneys."[11] The IMS offers a program called Jurisight, which helps attorneys to valuably incorporate mindfulness into their legal practices by helping them to deal with what is, even if it's unexpected, and by helping them to deal with their colleagues, clients, witnesses, and even their adversaries in a more genuine and more present manner, and to focus on people and situations with consistent clarity.

Some life lessons that we can learn best in the legal profession

What better way is there to learn about what justice really means and what it means for each of us than working in the legal industry? Plato had a lot of ideas about a lot of things, which were expressed in his approximately 750,000 written words. Many of these words were written about justice, and according to Plato, justice isn't just something that exists in a law court, at least occasionally. According to Plato, justice is a psychological phenomenon as well as a legal and a social one. This idea isn't theoretical or complicated at all, because ultimately if we are not getting natural life justice, we are getting unhappiness, through living in a state of fear or anger or misery. Justice means all of us being able to live well, and the legal profession can be a great opportunity to receive constant working reminders of the extremely valuable life lesson that justice doesn't mean taking freedom away from people; it means giving freedom to people—ourselves and others.

A mini interview with a mindful lawyer

Interviewer: What's the most important attribute of a good lawyer?

Mindful lawyer (at least occasionally!): The most significant skill for a lawyer is that of listening, careful listening. By doing so, a person is truly heard and only then can you be in a position to help.

Int: How might mindfulness help a person to work better and more enjoyably as a lawyer?

ML: Mindfulness can help lawyers to really listen. I used to think my job was "to know," but though experience and expertise in technical areas is required, actual listening—and not rehearsing an opinion, advice, or direction—allows a response to hit the mark.

Int: Do you have any anecdotes that might illustrate a mindful and/or mindless approach to working as a lawyer?

ML: The competitive field of law is these days more and more a business, and winning points/arguments against your "opponent" seems to be the norm, leaving the truth of the matter somewhat obscured. I have on many an occasion "won the contest" between us bull-at-a-gate lawyers (and felt extremely impressed with my deft skill) but pretty much left the client out of the equation. By simply listening and asking a few questions, a client often arrives at his or her own decision on an issue, resulting in me being thanked profusely when really all I did was listen to a story.

The healing industry

Healing yourself is connected with healing others.

—Yoko Ono

Healing really just means the restoration of our natural state—of health—by recognizing and doing whatever it takes to get there. The best way of dealing with healing is by not needing it, just as the best way of dealing with lawyers is by not needing them, but for those of us who need to be healed or to heal it's a wonderful opportunity to go straight to the core of our being. The healing industry includes health professionals and allied health professionals: doctors, nurses, vets, psychologists, medical specialists, physiotherapists, osteopaths, kinesiologists, and many, many more. The greater healing industry also includes all of the rest of us, who work at least occasionally in this universal industry even if only on ourselves.

What makes a good healer good and a good one better?

Being a good healer is a bit like being a good sculptor: good healers bring out what's real in people by helping them to eliminate what's unreal in them—the unnatural, unhelpful, unnecessary, and often infectious. A good healer is also like a good teacher in that nobody really heals anybody: a good healer helps people to heal themselves. A vital element of healing for the healer and for the patient is the recognition of what's right with people as well as what's wrong with them, and healing is optimally a process of working together with someone who needs it and who realizes that they need it.

Being a good healer is like being a good creative artist because an important aspect of healing is being able to keep seeing new ways of doing, new ways of being, new ways of overcoming, new ways of becoming. If people stay stuck in their mental and physical ruts, it's unlikely that they will ever have the quantum life shift that healing offers and comes from. As the great healer of cosmic uncertainty Albert Einstein once remarked, doing the same thing again and again and expecting a different result is insanity. Real healing is life healing, and to help people be well-healed, a good healer needs to recognize that they are doing far more than giving people a potion or a remedy that neither they nor their healing colleagues, including their patients, understands.

Real healing comes from real knowing—of what it is that makes us well and what it is that makes us unwell. Ultimately, a healer is a knower and experiencer of ultimate truth, the truth of who we really are and of who we really can be, so a healer is also a healer of ignorance and doubt. Healing comes from stilling the mind, body, and life circumstances to a single point where both the healer and patient can recognize what's really going on. Bad health isn't just bad luck; it's something that we always have an active involvement in—at some point in the illness chain of events—even if only at the stage of whether we decide to learn something from our illness or to succumb to it, all the way from our mind and body to our spirit. Good healers recognize the vital need for an active healing collaboration between the person they are healing and themselves.

A good gardener needs to grow themselves and a good rocket scientist or publicist needs to launch themselves. Even more importantly, a good healer needs to heal themselves. But don't worry if you're an official healer and it seems like you can't. Life is mysterious and wonderful and there are plenty of great healers who could heal many people except themselves. Great healing is like any other great work: its results don't matter; the intent itself is what makes greatness and what ultimately heals. The essential ingredient of a great healer is empathy, having enough access to our essential humanity to practically realize what John Donne said: "Do not send to know for whom the bell tolls, it tolls for thee." It's never too late to heal our spirit or others' spirit by recognizing that we are one and that we can help each other to be the best one that we can be.

Mindfulness and healing

There is plenty of scientific evidence that mindfulness can help to heal people with a wide range of physical, psychological, and life problems that can lead to a wide range of physical, psychological, and life illnesses. A lot of this evidence is presented in *Mindfulness for Life*.[12] There is also plenty of evidence that mindfulness can help healers to heal. Paradoxically, the healing professions can be the most stressful and to some extent this is due to our empathy: we inherently care that someone else is suffering and we often suffer as a result. There's nothing wrong with empathy, but it doesn't need to lead to suffering. If our empathy is so deep that we feel a oneness with others that transcends suffering and separation, then our empathy isn't our problem; it's our solution.

Mindfulness has been used to help the practitioners and students of a wide range of health professionals be healthier and happier, and to do their jobs better and more enjoyably, and with more sustainable empathy. The mindfulness programs offered to medical students at universities such as Monash and Deakin in Australia and at Harvard in the United States were mentioned in Chapter 1. There are also many other studies, such as the one conducted in California by Shauna Shapiro and others, which found that mindfulness programs improved the stress levels, quality of life (including working enjoyment), and self-compassion scores of a wide range of health professionals.[13]

Some life lessons that we can learn best as a mindful healer

Where better than in the healing professions can we learn that what we do to and for others we do to and for ourselves?

A mini interview with a mindful healer

Interviewer: What's the most important attribute of a good healer?

Mindful healer (at least occasionally!): "Groundedness" is a term that many healers use for being balanced, centered, present, and awakened. It is vital for any healer work, both in everyday life and during each and every session. In a practical sense, this term is interchangeable for mindfulness and is the most basic and practical quality of being a healer.

Int: How might mindfulness help healers to work better and more enjoyably?

MH: Mindfulness is essential to all aspects of healing. One's capacity as a healer is afforded by education, skill, and most importantly, an ability to address a client's needs—on a moment by moment basis. This would not be possible at all without mindfulness.

Int: Do you have any anecdotes that illustrate a mindful and/or a mindless approach to working as a healer?

MH: As a healer, I find that stress and anxiety play a major role in many health issues. Mindfulness is the most empowering tool to facilitate healing. There is most often very little stress in the present.

When I began working as a kinesiologist, I found that I felt totally drained after working with many people. I was wasting a lot of energy worrying about all sorts of things: were they enjoying the session, did they think I was a good enough practitioner, or even that a person's problem seemed so severe that I felt totally overwhelmed by all of their issues and didn't see an answer. Mindfulness allows me to let go of wasting attention and energy on worry and just get on with helping my clients as needed. I no longer feel drained by my work, but energized. Needless to say, the results for my clients have improved enormously.

Many years ago, I had a client who suffered terrible pain and swelling in most of his major joints. During his first kinesiology session, we discovered that he was constantly focusing his attention on the needs of others, putting his own needs last and automatically forgetting himself. The healing he needed was simply around focusing his mind on his body and the experience of being present with himself and "living in the now." He realized that he had been always distracted by what he thought others needed. After one session, his pain mostly went away, and after three sessions, it was totally gone. It was as if his body was trying to bring his attention back to the present, so that he could begin to know himself and express this in his life. Mindfulness is amazing.

Chapter 9

Mindfulness and Our Life Work

Enjoy your achievements as well as your plans. Keep interested in your own career, however humble; it is a real possession in the changing fortunes of time.
—Desiderata (reputedly found in St. Paul's Church, Baltimore, 1692; actually written by Max Ehrmann, 1927)

Most of us spend most of our time doing some kind of work, whether we like it or not. Work is a vital aspect of our lives and it can also be our greatest opportunity to achieve a profound working knowledge and to experience the complete peace and enjoyment that comes when we work out who we really are: connected, fulfilled, and happy. There's more to our working whole than the sum of our working parts, and we can realize the deeper value of work to our whole being when we realize that we don't work just to live, but also live to work...on ourselves. This doesn't mean that we were born to be whatever it is that we're working at—whether that's a dishwasher, a tax accountant, a camel jockey, or whatever—but that whatever we're working at gives us a unique opportunity to go beyond it to find out what we're really working at and who we really are.

What really works for us?

Our jobs can do much more for us and for the people we're connected with than just help us to pay our household bills (enormously helpful though this might be!). Our jobs can also help us to pay our cosmic bills—repaying our individual life investment by re-connecting to its source. Our real work isn't what we do in our jobs; it's what we do in ourselves. Once we work out who we really are, it's relatively easy to find out what job works best for us and how best to do it.

To do any job as well and as rewardingly as we can, we need to understand a greater practical reality than just how we can work best at a mechanical level, and we need to understand a greater human reality than just who we think we are. Our greater reality consists of the total picture of all the people, situations, and events that we experience, and not just the bits of the picture that we're fleetingly interested in. Psychologists like to show people stuff that they think helps them think, but at least some of the stuff that psychologists like to show people can help them to do more than just think; it can help them to know.

A gestalt is a picture that we can perceive in different ways; a well-known example is a picture that is either of an old woman or a young woman wearing a scarf, depending on how we see it or work it out. It's the same picture, but how we see it can change. A common working example of a gestalt is when something happens that we call an interruption to our work. Because we've seen what happened as "an interruption," this is the picture of it that we've created. We could also see the situation as a welcome opportunity to do something unexpected and valuable, and possibly as a welcome opportunity to help someone who needs our help. The real meaning of any gestalt, including human life and human working life, is that our answer is the total picture, not just the bits of it that we're stuck on.

Our true working reality, like our true living reality, includes not just our big picture but our huge picture—of all the people and situations to which we are connected, including our customers, colleagues, underlings, and even our bosses! Our work gives us a vital opportunity to reach a higher and more connected consciousness, which gives us a macro life and working-life perspective far greater than the micro perspectives that can upset us so much.

Small picture workplace catastrophes such as hammering our thumbnail instead of our gang nail, or putting antelope rather than cantaloupe in the vegetarians' fruit salad, don't force us to get upset. They just give us an opportunity to get upset. We can choose to rise above our attachments to what only looks like our ultimate reality, and instead do the opposite of getting upset. With the right mindfulness set, our jobs are a portal to an unshakeable understanding of our life, our work, and our life work as something deeply right and valuable. With the right mindfulness set, we can see ourselves as an integral part of a vast working whole rather than just a working pimple that wants to be promoted to a boil. Our jobs are a wonderful opportunity for us to see our particular place in the magnificent cosmic creation, and they are constantly flashing cosmic connection messages at us in neon lights…if we take off our mind-made dark glasses and just see the light: "You are here! You are now! This is it!"

Working mindfulness can help us to understand not only where we are and who we are, but also where we are going and why.

Working our way to enlightenment

In Pali, the language of Gautama the Buddha, Dhamma means "The Way of Truth." This word is spelled Dharma in the Sanskrit language, but however we spell it or pronounce or define it, the ability to find our natural and right way, and follow it is vital to our life success and to our working-life success. We can't follow someone else's natural and right way and expect to find our home base of natural peace, fulfilment, and optimal productivity. We can't beg, borrow, or steal. We can only recognize it and our own way there, and follow it. When referring to Dhamma, the spiritual teacher Eknath Easwaran wrote, "In the sphere of human activity, probably no word is richer in its connotations. Dharma is behavior that is in line with…unity."[1]

Would you rather get a fabulous pay raise that would allow you to buy a new house, or have a spouse so seemingly irresistible that other people will envy you, or would you rather get nothing more than what you have right now—on the outside—but have so much peace, contentment, and joy on the inside that you don't care if you have any more external stuff or what anyone else thinks? This is what enlightenment is. Or if you prefer a psychological term for the same state rather than a spiritual one, then try on for size the psychologist Abraham Maslow's well-known term "self-actualization." Both words mean the same thing: actually finding our real self and then actualizing it—doing something with it, working with it, lighting up with the joy of it.

Being enlightened or self-actualized or permanently at peace and happy without an external reason doesn't mean we have to take off to a cave and feel smug there about having what most people don't. There's actually something extremely practical about being in a state of "beyond mind," because in it we break into life's real value, rather than unsuccessfully trying to break out of its opposite. In our natural, ultimately mindful state, we know ourselves so completely that we also know others completely, and we are highly valuable to others as well as to ourselves. Working enlightenment is a much greater and more valuable thing than theoretical enlightenment, and we can work our way toward it by freeing ourselves of our mind-made distractions and treating our present work, whatever it is, as a gift. Being mindful can help us to unwrap our working gifts by helping us to recognize that something wrapped up in plain brown lunch paper or plain work clothes can be far greater than something wrapped up in the glitter of expectations.

The first simple but profound steps toward the mind- and heart-broadening possibilities of employing mindfulness at work are:

- Being aware and accepting of what we are working on, no matter what we think.
- Treating others as we would like to be treated, no matter what we think of them.
- Helping ourselves work toward where we need to get by helping others work toward where they need to get.

A consequence and also a driver of our mindful oiling of our rusty working parts is that as our working state of consciousness progresses, so does our working conscience. In higher states of working mindfulness, we are less likely to rationalize our working life dysfunctions, such as by attempting to justify work practices that benefit our interests at the expense of other people's interests. In higher states of working consciousness, we are less likely to think that our working ends justify our working means. There might indeed be a sucker born every minute, as the showman P.T. Barnum once noted. A mindful and heartful attitude to our work, however, will help us to realize that the real suckers are those of us who don't realize our connectedness, and who try to profit from the equivalent of their left hand pulling the wool over their right eye.

If the huge practical benefits of working mindfulness still sound idealistic or esoteric or a long way off or like something that will work only for other people, then please try a simple thought experiment. Think of a situation when you worked mindfully—with full attention and acceptance—and now think of one when you didn't, when you were distracted from what you were doing by what you would have liked to be doing. Which situation felt better, once your ego tidal wave subsided far enough to expose your universal reason?

What does an enlightened workplace look like?

It might seem like the only enlightened workplaces are monasteries up mountains, but there are actually some very ordinary examples of some very extraordinary and extraordinarily high profile people who have incorporated some enlightened work practices and possibilities into their organizations. Richard Branson, founder and chairman of the Virgin Group, helped to start a worldwide council of Elders that aims to bring some practical sanity into the working world. Australian entrepreneur Dick Smith has introduced large-scale lines of local products with a local conscience into supermarkets despite fierce opposition from competitors. Oprah Winfrey made much more than just fame and billions of dollars by publicly championing people she believed in to far greater acceptance and influence than they would have achieved without her help, such as Barack Obama and Eckhart Tolle.

When we work mindfully, our minds and our hearts open out to the ultimate reality of our human situation—and this means the ultimate working reality of who we are really connected to, what we are really working on, and how to really get the best working outcome for everyone. No matter how big we think the organization we work for is, what we are really working for is The Universe, Inc. When we work mindfully, we can realize that nobody lives or works alone, no matter what we think. Even if we think that we are the most dispensable employee of Harry's Fish and Chip Emporium, or the most senior employer at Manangatang Megamarketing Inc., we are all working this life shift together.

Working mindfully works because it helps us to work more successfully and enjoyably. Mindfulness is just a word that describes what we already have: a life essence and a life purpose. Now it's time to put this book down and put your thoughts about it away—filed under "F" for finished. Now it's time to stop "working" and just do, now. And just be, always.

Notes

Chapter 1

1. S. McKenzie and C. Hassed, *Mindfulness for Life* (Wollombi, Australia: Exisle Publishing, 2011).
2. Ibid., p. 7.

Chapter 3

1. D. Goleman, *Emotional Intelligence* (New York: Bantam Books, 1995).
2. Ibid.
3. J. Kabat-Zinn and D. Goleman, *Mindfulness @ Work: A Leading with Emotional Intelligence Conversation with Jon Kabat-Zinn.* (CD).

Chapter 4

1. *Macquarie Concise Dictionary (4th Ed.)*, Macquarie Dictionary Publishers, Sydney, 2006.
2. R. Webster, *The Seven Secrets of Success* (St. Paul: Llewellyn Publications, 1997).
3. T.H. Lawrence, *Seven Pillars of Wisdom* (Oxford, 1922).
4. G. Miller, "The Magical Number Seven, Plus or Minus Two: Some limits on our capacity for processing information," *Psychological Review,* Vol. 63(2), 1956, pp. 81–97.

5. M. Collins and C. Tamarkin, *Marva Collins Way: Returning to excellence in education* (New York: Penguin Putnam Inc., 1990).

6. E. Langer, T. Russell, and N. Eisenkraft, "Orchestral Performance and the Footprint of Mindfulness," *Psychology of Music*, Vol. 37 (2), April 2009, pp. 125–136.

Chapter 5

1. A. Fuller, *Tricky People* (Sydney: Finch Publishing, 2009).

2. S. McKenzie, *Vital Statistics* (Sydney: Elsevier, 2013).

3. T. Glomb, M. Duffy, J. Bono, and T. Yang, "Mindfulness at Work," *Research in Personnel and Human Resources Management*, Vol. 30, 2011, pp. 115–157.

4. E. Dane, "Paying Attention to Mindfulness and its Effects on Task Performance in the Workplace," *Journal of Management*, Vol. 37, July 2011, pp. 997–1018.

5. S. Shapiro, J. Astin, S. Bishop, and M. Cordova, "Mindfulness-Based Stress Reduction for Health Care Professionals: Results from a randomized trial," *International Journal of Stress Management*, Vol. 12, No. 2, 2005, pp. 164–176.

6. "College students losing their sensitive side," *Washington Post*, 31 May 2010, *www.washingtonpost.com*.

7. M. Argyle, F. Alkema, and R. Gilmour, "The Communication of Friendly and Hostile Attitudes by Verbal and Non-verbal Signals," *European Journal of Social Psychology*, Vol. 1(3), 1971, pp. 385–402.

Chapter 6

1. C. Spearman, "'General intelligence,' Objectively Determined and Measured," *American Journal of Psychology*, Vol. 15, 1904, pp. 201–293.

2. L. Hudson, *Contrary Imaginations: A psychological study of the English schoolboy* (Harmondsworth: Penguin, 1967).

3. E. De Bono, *Lateral Thinking: Creativity Step by Step*, (New York: Harper & Row, 1970).

4. R. Yerkes and J. Dodson, "The Relation of Strength of Stimulus to Rapidity of Habit-formation," *Journal of Comparative Neurology and Psychology*, Vol. 18, 1908, pp. 459–482.

5. D. Meadows, *Leverage Points: Places to intervene in a system* (Hartland, Vt.: The Sustainability Institute, 1999).

6. Ibid.

7. B.H. Gunaratana, *Mindfulness in Plain English* (Somerville, Mass.: Wisdom Publications, 2002).

8. F. Nietzsche, *On the Use and Abuse of History for Life* (A. Collins, Trans.) (New York: MacMillan, 1957). Originally published in 1874.

9. Meadows, op. cit.

10. B. Ostafin and K. Kassman, "Stepping out of History: Mindfulness improves insight problem solving," *Consciousness and Cognition* Vol. 21, 2012, pp. 1031–1036.

11. M. Gladwell, *Blink: The power of thinking without thinking*, (New York: Black Bay Books, 2007).

12. J. Surowiecki, *The Wisdom of Crowds* (New York: Anchor Books, 2005).

Chapter 7

1. L. Wankel, "The Importance of Enjoyment to Adherence and Psychological Benefits from Physical Activity," *International Journal of Sport Psychology*, Vol. 24(2), Apr–Jun 1993, Special issue: Exercise and Psychological Wellbeing, pp. 151–169.

2. M. Killingsworth and D. Gilbert, "A Wandering Mind is an Unhappy Mind," *Science*, Vol. 330, No. 6006, 12 November 2010, p. 932.

3. G.J. Boyle and J.M. Joss-Reid, "Relationship of Humour to Health: A psychometric investigation," *British Journal of Health Psychology*, Vol. 9 (Pt 1), February 2004, pp. 51–66.

Chapter 8

1. J. Ritchie, "Mindfulness and Your Business," 2012 *http://theentertainingbusiness.com/2012/07/20/ mindfulness-and-your-business/*.

2. M. Seligman, *Helplessness: On depression, development, and death* (San Francisco: W.H. Freeman, 1975).

3. M. Seligman, *Learned Optimism* (New York: Simon & Shuster, 1990).

4. D. Schoeberlein, *Mindful Teaching and Teaching Mindfulness* (Somerville, Mass.: Wisdom Publications, 2009).

5. M. Crawford, *The Case for Working with Your Hands* (New York: Viking, 2009).

6. R. Pirsig, *Zen and the Art of Motorcycle Maintenance* (New York: William Morrow and Company, 1974).

7. E. Herrigel, *Zen in the Art of Archery* (New York: Pantheon Books, 1973). First published in Germany in 1948.

8. Pirsig, op. cit.

9. Herrigel, op. cit.

10. *www.law.berkeley.edu/mindfulness.htm*.

11. *http://imslaw.com/Home.html*.

12. S. McKenzie and C. Hassed, *Mindfulness for Life* (Wollombi, Australia: Exisle Publishing, 2012).

13. S. Sapiro, J. Astin, S. Bishop, and M. Cordova, "Mindfulness-based Stress Reduction for Health

Care Professionals: Results from a randomized trial," *International Journal of Stress Management* Vol. 12, No. 2, 2005, pp. 164–176.

Chapter 9

1. E. Easwaran, *The Dhammapada* (Blue Mountain Center of Meditation, 1987) p. 24.

Index

About the Author

Dr. Stephen McKenzie has more than 20 years' experience in researching and teaching a broad range of psychological areas, including depression, dementia, substance abuse, and most recently, mindfulness. He has a unique ability as a lecturer, researcher, and writer to present potentially complex information in a warm, engaging, and entertaining way. Dr. McKenzie has recently been appointed as the Research and Evaluation Officer for the *Healthy Together* Geelong Preventive Health Project and is providing research support to help improve the health of Geelong residents. Together with Dr. Craig Hassed, he is the author of the highly successful *Mindfulness for Life*.